THE I DODGER

by
Albert F Darlington

Published by
Laundry Cottage Books

Kenneth JS Ballantyne
Laundry Cottage
Shawbirch Road
Admaston
Wellington
Shropshire
TF5 0AD

Tel. & Fax: 01952 – 223931
email: cenneach@westcoast13.wanadoo.co.uk

First published in Great Britain in 2006 by
Laundry Cottage Books,
Laundry Cottage, Shawbirch Road, Admaston,
Wellington, Shropshire, TF5 0AD.

Contents

Foreword

I attempted to write this book forty years ago but was unable to cope with the typewriter. The computer has solved that problem and because I kept most of my notes, I decided to have another stab at it. I was also determined to make it all my own work so no ghosting was allowed but I do admit that my daughters sometimes looked over my shoulder and said, "No Dad, you can't say that."

Most of the chapters deal with the war years and the reader must bear in mind that this is the view of an underage private soldier. I may have been the youngest soldier on active service (very active service) in the British Army. I saw a News clipping about an Australian soldier whose father, also in the Services, spotted him in Burma, reported him and had him sent home. He was two months older than me so I might hold the Commonwealth title as well.

My attempt to keep a diary failed miserably after a few days in action but all the events here are true, only the names, places and dates gave me any trouble. It was not just a case of not knowing where you were but what you were supposed to be doing. The infantry soldier never had the complete picture; this is made absolutely clear in Chapter 15. The event is very vivid in my mind and for years I thought I had been wounded on the River Po. I am indebted to the Regimental Archivists of the Oxford and Buckingham Light Infantry at Slade Park for their help.

My apologies to all the officers and men I haven't been able to name with any certainty. I think the officer with the Verey Light pistol in Chapter 8 was Lieutenant Hamilton and the CO in Chapter 14 was probably Major Montgomery but I can't be sure.

Finally, I must thank my daughter Barbara for her help in sorting out the computer glitches that cropped up and confused the unsophisticated author like myself.

AFD

The Severn Hospice

Part of the proceeds from the sale of this book will be donated to the Severn Hospice.

Severn Hospice cares for patients from Shropshire and Mid Wales with life-limiting illnesses including cancer, motor neurone disease and multiple sclerosis. We strive to provide the highest standards of nursing and medical care, to sustain quality of life and dignity and to provide patients with relief from pain. To the families, friends and carers of our patients we extend the same loving support, help and counselling, as such illnesses affect whole families

The Hospice helps its patients enjoy a better quality of life, often enabling them to do things they thought had gone forever. It is not just a place where people go to die: many patients benefit from day hospice care and others return home following a period as an inpatient.

Jessica Darlington spent the last month of her life in the Hospice and died there on Good Friday, 2001. The care and tranquillity which she experienced at the Hospice, and the support which was given to her husband Albert and their family was so important to them.

We are mostly reliant upon, and deeply grateful for, the contributions and generosity of people in finding the money to keep functioning effectively and moving forward each year.

In this respect, we are very grateful to Albert for his support by donating part of the proceeds from the sale of this book and thank you for helping us by buying Albert's story.

Lucy Proctor
Fundraising Manager
Severn Hospice
June 2006

Registered charity number 512394

The D-Day Dodger

In 1944, Lady Nancy Astor, the first woman MP to take her seat in the House of Commons, made a speech in which she infamously insulted the British soldiers fighting in the Italian Campaign by referring to them as 'the D-Day Dodgers'. This song was written by soldiers of the British Eighth Army as a sarcastic reply to Lady Astor. Sung to the tune of *Lili Marlene*.

1 We are the D-Day Dodgers, out in Italy,
Always on the vino, always on the spree
Eighth Army skivers and their tanks,
We go to war in ties like swanks,
We are the D-Day Dodgers, in sunny Italy.

2 We landed at Salerno, a holiday with pay
Jerry brought his bands out to cheer us on our way,
Showed us the sights and gave us tea,
We all sang songs, the beer was free,
We are the D-Day Dodgers, in sunny Italy.

3 Palermo and Cassino were taken in our stride
We didn't go to fight there, we just went for the ride.
Anzio and Sangro are just names,
We only went to look for dames,
We are the D-Day Dodgers, in sunny Italy.

4 On our way to Florence we had a lovely time,
We drove a bus from Rimini, right through the Gothic Line,
Then to Bologna we did go
And went bathing in the River Po
We are the D-Day Dodgers, in sunny Italy.

5 We hear the boys in France are going home on leave
After six months service it's a shame they're not relieved
But we can carry on out here
For what may be a few more years
We are the D-Day Dodgers, in sunny Italy.

6 Once we heard a rumour that we were going home
Back to dear old Blighty, never more to roam,
Then someone said, "In France you'll fight",
We answered, "No, we'll just sit tight",
The windy D-Day Dodgers, in sunny Italy.

7 Dear Lady Astor, you think you know a lot,
Standing on a platform and talking tommy rot,
Dear England's sweetheart and her pride
We think you mouth is much too wide
From the D-Day Dodgers, in sunny Italy.

8 Look around the hillsides, in the mud and rain
See the scattered crosses, some which have no name,
Heartbreak and toil and suffering gone,
The lads beneath them slumber on,
They are the D-Day Dodgers who'll stay in Italy.

Chapter 1

Hollywood has a lot to answer for

The war started when I was thirteen years old. Imagine what this meant to a boy brought up on action comics and air guns, with a third rate education and who thought he was tough. Before the war, the Army and Navy accepted boys but there would be no action; 'powder monkeys' in the Navy were a thing of the past and who wanted to be an Army drummer boy! No: get to the shooting war. I know now that this is romantic nonsense and probably fuelled by Hollywood movies; but I was a kid.

At fourteen I had to start work. A local butcher, for whom I did some Saturday work, offered me a full time job but that didn't appeal to me in the least. I knew the butcher well: he had a brother with a farm outside Birmingham and I used to shoot rabbits there regularly. I was into gun culture long before they coined the phrase. Engineering sounded more up my street, so I started an apprenticeship as a toolmaker. At the firm advice came thick and fast. The old hands came up with the answer; the Merchant Navy: plenty of action there, son. They would smile when they said it; they did not think I was serious. As the country was on a war footing, all the rules had changed. The factory could not give me the sack for misbehaviour, only suspension; but you could not leave your job either, except to join the Forces: the factory would have to put up with my antics. My wage at the factory was fourteen shillings (seventy pence) a week, but in a few months, with one pound in my pocket, I hitched down to Bristol.

I should mention my parents at this point. Apart from the ten shillings a week they got for my keep, they didn't give a damn and that's how I wanted it. I was confident; Bristol here I come.

When I arrived at the port, I was in the wrong place as I had to get to Avonmouth. When I eventually arrived there it was late and in the blackout it was impossible to find anything. I ended up asking complete strangers where I could get a cheap bed for the night. I was so at risk at this point that it was only my naivety that saved me from being scared to death. I finished up at the Seamen's Mission at one shilling a night. It was my first and last night in a 'doss house'. I had not led a sheltered life but the performance after lights out was unbelievable. We slept in a large dormitory with beds on either side of the room. First came the drunks, singing and shouting, waking those already asleep. Then someone started to get into a bed already occupied and a fight started. It finished up with a coloured man brandishing a large knife, chasing another seaman, who was leaping the beds like a champion hurdler. They rushed out of the room and then came back with one of them bleeding badly. The police were called and they treated everyone like criminals. I checked out at daybreak.

Acting on more reliable information, I turned up at the Seamen's Rest. The proprietor was a little cautious at first - the place was strictly for seamen - but I managed to convince him that it was only a matter of hours before I would be wearing sea boots. By comparison with the last place, the Seamen's Rest was posh. The door from the street opened onto a large room with two billiard tables, a long counter, plenty of lounge chairs and a small restaurant. There was no open plan dormitory this time, but a series of small rooms, built like cages. We may have looked like monkeys but they were civilized enough to contain a bed and a locker each.

"This will do me for a few days," I thought, "until I get sorted."

The Rest was a mine of information, good and bad. You had to be in the Seamen's Union to get a ship and you could not get a union card unless you had been to sea. Catch 22. (I believe that actors still have the same problem). I was finally told, "There is a war on, and maybe the rules have been relaxed, go to the Pool Office and find out." This was very good advice.

The Merchant Navy Pool Office was on the way to the docks: a road I would come to know so well over the next few days. The office was full of rumours about convoys that had arrived during the night and convoys that were about to arrive but the Office clerks overruled the Lords of the Admiralty.
"Sorry, no ships. Difficult to place untrained boys. Look in on the morrow."

I looked in on the morrow and every other morrow for the next few days and finally ran out of money. Just as the money situation got serious and it became known at the Rest, I was approached by a person who said it was no trouble to get a ship if you knew the right person. He would take me to Bristol to see the Captain and pay my fare. This generosity did not make me suspicious; I thought they would take the money out of my first month's pay. On the way to Bristol, I studied my companion carefully and doubts began to form. Was he the sort of person who had Captains for friends? I had this over-confidence in my own ability to take care of myself in any situation, so I went along, into the back alleys and slums of the city.

Finally, in a back room I met 'The Captain'. All my schoolboy impressions of sailing before the mast disappeared: whatever these characters had in store for me, it was not life on the ocean wave. If they had made some effort - a uniform, a peaked cap, or a bit of gold braid - they could have sold me the scam but there was no way I was going to go along with this scruffy loser. I gave the moron the answers he wanted to hear, until arrangements were made to move me somewhere else. Once outside the room I waited for my chance. If it came to a punch up, how would I fare? My minder was slightly bigger than me but very unfit; if I could make a run for it, he would have no chance. I waited until we were out of the back streets: Nelson Road, I still remember it: how poetic. Nelson was only twelve years old when he went to sea, but his road was nice and long. With a few choice expletives in the face of my so-called benefactor, I was off like a rabbit. He attempted to give chase but there was no hope for him. Running was my thing. About three miles down the road, I considered my options: no good going back to Avonmouth as I was skint. Give up and go home but first, how to get a lift back to Birmingham and in the future pay more attention to the stories in the News of the World.

The difficulty back home was not with my parents but in the factory. I may have been a daft bugger to some but the younger employees were being influenced by my actions. One friend in particular paid serious attention and a few months later he was off on the same tour. Imagine my anger and surprise when I learnt from his mother that Charlie was somewhere at sea. This will not do; the war has been on for eighteen months and it can't last much longer. I was fifteen and still nowhere. My wages were now eighteen shillings (ninety pence) a week, so getting enough money together was a serious issue.

One of the boys in the factory owed me two shillings on a bet and was refusing to pay. The kid had a nickname of Nazi because he was no good; and what's more he was bigger than me so I needed a dirty trick to change the odds. The opportunity came when he reached for his overalls. All the lower orders of the factory wore bib and brace or boiler suits for protective clothing; only toolmakers or foremen wore cow gowns. There was a definite class system and a big divide between office and factory but everyone knew their place. My place, at this moment, was to get the money this no-good welcher owed me. When you put on a boiler suit, there is an awkward moment when you have to force the garment over your shoulders after you have put your arms in. When he was in this semi-helpless position I rushed him and he was down, with me beating down on his face. He agreed to pay up but it was too late as the blood was up and I kept going. A foreman hearing the commotion came over and pulled me off. The foreman who came to the rescue was a well-known bookie, not only in the factory but also all round the area.

I shall digress for a moment while I explain the ridiculous betting laws we had to put up with. Betting outside the racecourse was illegal, toffs were allowed to bet by telephone and have accounts but us plebs had to use street bookies: strictly no credit. The foreman who saved the welcher from further damage, was a well-known bookmaker who worked at the factory. He had people collecting bets for him and they used 'a clock bag', a simple device to stop people placing bets after the race had started. As it was illegal, the police had to arrest somebody and they used to tip him off when they were coming. Mr Harrison would arrange for somebody else to be caught holding the bag. Someone with no previous convictions so the fine was small and Harry would cover all the expenses. I know it's laughable but that's how it was. When we put our bets in the clock bag, we would sign them with a nom de plume like Mickey Mouse or Guy Fawkes, just in case the police tried to prove some kid was having sixpence each way on Lucky Lad.

Back to the problem of the two shillings: when Mr Harrison heard all the facts it was ok, he had no time for welchers either so nothing was said to the management. All this shows how concerned I was about money and getting to Avonmouth. Whilst I was saving up I made a knuckleduster, copied from the latest gangster movie. It is a serious piece of kit and I still have it and although I can't get it on my hand now, it's in my collection of memorabilia.

My past experience had taught me a great deal and I had to get it right this time. I had saved four pounds, which should have been enough for a month. I made the hike to Avonmouth in record time. The proprietor of the Seamen's Rest was not surprised to see me, he had assumed I had been at sea and I did not tell him the full story. His young daughter had started to work in the restaurant so I had another reason to put on a good show. I settled down to a routine: twice a day to the Pool Office and play snooker with Connie in between cups of tea and buns; it went on and on.

My hopes began to wane, two weeks and nothing. The Pool Office routine was wearing thin. I didn't even go up to the clerk; I put my head round the door he would look up and wave me away. Then it happened, expecting dismissal I had already turned away when he shouted and waved a paper at me. I couldn't contain myself, winning first prize must be something like this and I rushed up to the counter.
"Get down to the Empire Cabot straight away. Cabin boy wanted."

Out in the street I started to run and then I thought, "You are not catching a bus; you are a member of the Merchant Marine." By the time I got to the dock policeman, I was blasé. He pointed me in the right direction and there it was all twelve thousand tons of it, the Empire Cabot. What a grand name for such a scruffy ship. It was being loaded with ballast. Why a ship should carry rocks around in the hold was a mystery to me at the time but every time a load crashed down, clouds of dust would rise up and settle all over the deck. To find out, I went up the gangplank. On board there was a man in a peaked cap directing the loading.

"Glad to be aboard sir. I'm the new cabin boy, sir. Says so on this paper sir." All the 'sirs' were wasted, he had no rank.

"Forecastle," he said pointing down the deck. The next seaman took me below, showed me a cupboard with a cot and explained the situation.

"The regular boy hasn't turned up yet, so this will be your cabin. We got on to the Pool Office to be on the safe side. If he shows up before we sail you're out."

"When are we sailing, sir?"

"You don't ask those sort of questions. There's a war on."

The rest of the day, there was nothing to do except familiarize myself with the ship. I didn't dare go ashore because I was so unsure of things that if I lost contact the whole ship would disappear. Aft, forward, port, starboard, bilge, an educational day and so to bed in the cupboard. I lay there fully clothed, my night attire still at the Rest. I was hoping not to have to return there as I still owed a few shillings. I'll see to that when I have been round the world. There was little sleep that night, my mind was racing. What about a uniform? Apparently, you could wear what you liked, even dress up like an admiral if you didn't mind being laughed at. A nice blue square rig, with a white cap and a gold anchor on the front, that should do. I must check out the cost. I am going to be on £28 a month with heavy stoppages.

I was up early in the morning and there was a different sound to the ship. I wandered around the deck; maybe they were about to sail. I was still starving, it seemed as though they never ate, the galley was closed I was told. Then a group of people approached, there was a boy with them. I hoped they were not coming to the ship, but they stepped on to the gangway. The boy had a kitbag on his shoulder and he strode across the deck like an old sea dog and disappeared below. I made myself invisible, if we sailed straight away they may not notice that there were two of us, but ships don't behave like cars at a garage forecourt; within ten minutes the mate was looking for me.

"Right lad, hop it, let them know at the Pool Office for me."

I didn't say, "Yes sir," this time; I was not going to say 'sir' again to anyone, ever. The Pool Office just said bad luck, try again tomorrow. Connie at the Rest was more sympathetic as I ate my first food in twenty-four hours. I was into my third week and the money situation was beginning to be a worry. I settled into the old routine and a few days later there was an incident in the washroom. The communal washroom at the Rest consisted of a row of basins in the centre and toilets at the end. I was washing my face and paid no attention to the man who came into the room. Jamming the door with a chair, he came over and grabbed me from behind. His intentions were obvious and I kicked out viciously. I was wearing heavy shoes and struck him on the shins; this was a big guy and he was angry. He used his fists and knocked me under the washbasins which were supported by iron frames. I held on to the iron struts and when he tried to pull me out, I kicked, scratched and shouted at the top of my voice. It attracted attention and soon there were people outside the door. The manager and another man forced their way in and then one hell of a fight started.

When things calmed down the manager took me downstairs to sort it out. I wanted the police but he didn't want them involved. He said I could forget the few shillings that I still owed on the tab. This cheered me up and he realized this was the way to stop me from making too much fuss.

"Well if I can have another week I am certain to get a ship by then".

He agreed to this but as an afterthought he asked me to go and get my overcoat. Puzzled I did as I was told and handed the coat over; he took it and locked it in a cupboard. I thought this was strange and then I realized that he was covering himself as the coat was worth at least eight pounds. With my newly acquired credit I could have luxuries like egg or beans on toast and I noticed that Connie was making notes and the normal freebies had stopped. The rest of the time it was back to the old routine, beating a path to the Pool Office.

I don't know what stage the depression hit but I realized as I entered the fourth week this could not go on. God knows what I owed for my bed and board. As I went to bed that night I decided that the Pool Office had given me their last rejection. In the early hours of the morning I decided to go home. I dressed, packed my bits and pieces and went down stairs. The place was quiet and dark; I crept behind the bar to collect my overcoat. The locked cupboard was not a serious problem, a few good pulls on the door and it was open. The front door to the building was screened off with blackout material leaving a space about six feet square. I pulled the curtain aside, I was under a bit of nervous tension and when I saw a man sitting there I stepped back quickly and waited for trouble. He must have heard me break open the cupboard; it never occurred to me they would have a night watchman. It seemed like hours but nothing stirred; I had another peep. Head back, legs straight out, he was fast asleep. I gave a sigh of relief and sat down in the cafe to gather my thoughts. I had a choice, rush past him open the door out into the street and run: but what if the door was difficult and I lost time? I chose the alternative and so softly, softly I moved round him and tried the door; my luck was in, it was only on the catch and opening it enough to squeeze through, I stepped into the street.

There was a war on and a kid wandering the street in the early hours soon attracted the attention of a lone policeman. After he had checked I was only carrying dirty washing, I told him my story. The police in my neighbourhood were always the enemy, but this guy was a gem.

"Birmingham," he said, "follow me," and we went up to the main road. "Wait there. I will give you a shout when I'm ready."

I stood on the corner and watched him stop several lorries. Finally, one seemed to fit the bill. The big articulated lorry stood there, thumping away, whilst the copper held the cab door open.

"Come on son," he called. I could see by the look on the driver's face that all was not well.

"Just drop him off in the Midlands, that's all you've got to do."

He gave me a shove up and shut the door. The driver gave me one more glare and moved off. After about twenty minutes he stopped, got out of the cab and went to the rear. I slid over into his seat and watched him in the mirror. He was talking to a woman, waving his arms about and pointing to the front. Now I could see it all; the long face, the aggravation. I couldn't hear what was being said but I can guess that the conversation went something like this:

"I've got this kid in the cab. I can't throw him out because the coppers have put him on to me and they may have taken my number. Leave it 'till I come back."

With a final wave of his arms, she walked away and he headed for the cab. I got back in my own seat as far to the nearside as possible. He slammed the door so hard the rig shook. With a final glare he crashed the gears and moved off. I sat in silence with my hand deep in my overcoat pocket and my fingers through the knuckleduster.

Travelling in wartime Britain was quite a unique experience. There were no signs and no lights; the illumination allowed on the vehicle was so little that it was difficult to go more than twenty miles an hour. Army convoys used motorcycle outriders to make it easier. We had no such escorts, so we plodded on in unfriendly silence until daybreak. I was half asleep when he shouted,
"This is it, I can't drive into town."

We were near the Austin factory at Longbridge, so it would be no problem for a streetwise kid like me to get from Northfield to Erdington on the other side of the city. I didn't feel like any more smart arsing and I still had a few pennies in my pocket so I decided to go home in style, on the tram.
My arrival back home was greeted with the usual,
"You're back again are you?"

Perhaps I had better explain the reason for this off hand interest in my well being. I had a stepmother and she was my second stepmother. The first one was a terror and she used to knock me about. On my first day at school, before my fifth birthday, I was led home by a knowledgeable six year old, (parents didn't collect their children in those days). I was nervous and had shit my trousers. My Nan, I never called her mom, dragged me out in to the yard and scrubbed me with a yard bush with bristles like steel. My shoulders were bleeding and a neighbour had to stop her from killing me. She was a lot older than my father and she made his life a misery too. She died of cancer which may have been the reason for her strange behaviour, but I had to put up with it until I was eight years old.

The next two years were the best time of my school days; Dad would disappear at eight o'clock in the morning and leave me to get myself off to school and arrange my own meals. I became an expert in rice puddings. If I was brought home by a policeman for a misdemeanour, I knew that there was no one at home to do anything about it and the police never followed it up. This came to an end when my father re-married. Step-mom two was a lot younger than my father and wanted a child of her own. I was too big and tough to be treated as before so she took no interest in me and we tolerated each other. I never called her mom, I gave her no title at all and I made sure I never needed her.

Soon after I returned from Avonmouth, I joined the Army Cadets. Well they have rifle drill and Sergeants shouting in my face didn't worry me. The nearest I ever came to any action was the nightly bombing. We lost all our tiles and windows on one occasion when a bomb dropped at the end of the road. I was the first one into the hole and found a piece of hot shrapnel. I was taking it home when a man took it off me; he said kids couldn't have things like that. I followed him down the road heaping abuse on him. "He's got my souvenir," I shouted, but nobody took any notice; everyone had their own problems.

I had to go back to work at the factory where there were some exciting moments, like when Fred came. A new works engineer started and the management decided to put me with him as his gofer. We didn't have a proper office, just a corner of the factory with a screen round a bench. He was a very interesting man, anything electrical or mechanical he could fix. His name was Fred Taylor and he was full of surprises.

One morning I clocked in and everyone was talking.
"Have you seen that about your gaffer in the Daily Mirror?"
I couldn't wait to find out what the paper had to say and was just as amazed as everyone else. There on the front page was Fred swinging a propeller on an aircraft. The caption read, *"Man with his own aeroplane can't join the RAF as a pilot."* Fred was on the office staff so he didn't come in until nine o'clock and so I had to

wait another hour to find out what it was all about. Fred told me the whole story; he was a year too old to be taken on for pilot training and the RAF had strict rules.

"But what about the plane?" I asked.

"I made that myself, come over on Sunday to my place and I'll show it to you."

He lived at a place called Barr Beacon, a nice bike ride through green fields on a Sunday; I was feeling good. When I got there he was messing with a little Austin Seven.

"Get in, I'll take you up to the stable right away."

I didn't ask what the stables had to do with it; I was too excited. We drove high onto the beacon and parked outside a stable block. When he opened the doors, I was disappointed. Disappointed because I didn't know what to expect, I had been romancing with the idea that he might let me have a go at flying it. He pushed the fuselage outside I could see the wing stacked against the inside wall.

"But the newspaper said..."

He cut me off, "That's bullshit, look at this."

He went back into the stable and came out with the propeller. He slipped it on the spigot and stood with his hand on the prop.

"I put the wing on without fastening it down, there's your picture."

"You didn't fly it then?"

"I'm not allowed to, I've been grounded since 1939 that's why it's garaged up here."

I looked at newspaper clips of him flying high in the sky and one where he had crashed in a potato field without getting hurt. He could see my disappointment about not seeing it fly so he went into detail about how he made it. He couldn't get an engine light enough so he cast an aluminium one in his back garden using a home made furnace. The propeller he cut out of hardwood and it was beautifully finished. Shrinking canvas onto the main frame was child's play for a man of Fred's ability; he made it sound easy and I was so impressed.

"Come back to the house and I'll show you some really clever stuff."

When we got back, he took me into this large garden shed which was full of machinery like a factory tool-room. He took a contraption from a shelf and clamped it in the vice. He seemed very proud of this device and started to explain about guns. I was an Army Cadet and had been to lectures on the Bren gun so I understood what he was saying about automatic fire.

"You have to put the bullets in a belt or a magazine, I know about that," I said. He was so glad to have a genuine pupil and he got on with the show quickly.

"You've never seen anything like this before."

He screwed a funnel onto the mechanism in the vice, which I could now see was a magazine of a gun with trigger but no barrel or stock, then he took a box of point 22 cartridges from the shelf. I was very familiar with these small bullets which were easy to obtain and in use in every fair ground shooting gallery in the country; he poured some into the funnel.

"I can't fire it in the normal way, apart from the noise and blowing my shed to pieces, it would kill everyone in the neighbourhood."

I could see what he meant; you needed the explosion to blow the breach block back to pick up the next bullet for the repeat action. This was no problem for Fred, "I've connected it up to a compressed air bottle and removed the firing pin, so the action is the same," and he pulled the trigger.

Rat-a-tat-tat-tat-tat, the spent cartridges flew out all over the floor, I bent to pick them up and he tipped the rest of the box in, squeezed the trigger again and emptied the funnel.

Little did I know that within six months I would be doing the same thing for real but I never saw or heard of a hopper fed machine gun. Whenever I think of that garden shed I smile at present day health and safety regulations. Even I would agree it was a mite dangerous. As we walked to the house, he had a second thought,

"Before you go I've got one other thing to show you," and he went back into the shed and came out with a small boat and a large box.

His wife greeted us with a frosty look and some remarks about dinner being spoiled. Why wasn't this woman in awe of this man instead of moaning about trivialities? When she saw the boat she pulled a long face, slammed the kitchen door and shouted, "You're going to play with that thing all day, are you?"

"We're going to use the bathroom for ten minutes, that's all."

"Well don't mess it up like last time."

I couldn't understand this attitude not having any experience of watching normal married life.

He filled the bath with a few inches of water and floated the boat. After messing with the mystery box for a few minutes, he put a rolled up piece of silver paper in the boat like a mast, a bit more fiddling with the box and it started to hum. I watched boggle eyed as the boat moved up and down the bath. I know kids today have toys that will do this but sixty years ago I was watching pure magic. By the time I left to return home Fred had made a great impression on me, he was some engineer. Working together I heard about some of his problems and it's not surprising that he had a chip on his shoulder. His uninterested wife didn't help but it was mainly because he didn't have any paper qualifications. Without a degree no one would take him seriously and check what he was capable of. You would think a war would change all that but I took the trouble to find out what had happened to him. His nephew told me he did get into the RAF eventually but they put him in the RAF Regiment. To think a man of his talents guarding airports and marching up and down with the footsloggers, beggars belief. With people in authority making decisions like that, how did we win the war? When the hostilities ceased, he emigrated to Australia and when last heard of, he was opal mining. Get rich Fred, that's the best revenge.

I tried the Merchant Navy once again with a friend, but it wasn't a serious attempt. Straight down to Avonmouth, rejection by the Pool Office and back again. It was for the benefit of my pal Harold I was showing off, proving I knew the score. We were late getting back and had to sleep in a haystack for the night in Evesham. Harold's mother, father, sister and granddad never forgave me for exposing their offspring to such danger. It was 1942 and the war couldn't last much longer. The Army Cadets were no substitute for the real thing and I had to try again somewhere.

In the city centre there were recruiting offices for the Forces. I tried the Navy first; the Petty Officer (PO) decided to have a bit of fun with me.
"You are a tool maker are you, well you could be an artificer."
"What's that?" I said.
"Well you don't have to wear bell bottoms, you have a peaked cap like the captain and you drive the ship," he replied.
"Would I go abroad?"
"Ships don't go very well on land son, now sod off and get a birth certificate."
"I lost it," I tried, but he had heard it all before.
"Go round to the Registrar and get a copy."

The marines were in the same building, so I knocked on their door but the PO followed me in, had a word with the Sergeant and I was out. A few yards down the street there was an Army recruiting centre, so I went in. There was a different atmosphere in this office and these guys were keen. The recruiting Sergeant was friendly,

"I don't suppose you have a birth certificate?"

"No, I lost it," I pleaded again.

"Well don't worry about that for the moment."

This lifted my spirits to the roof.

"So how old are you?"

Now this was tricky; I had to add two years and one month to bring it up to eighteen years. That one month has caused me more trouble than the two years ever did.

The Sergeant went into action.

"When you sign your papers and accept the King's shilling there is no turning back."

"The King's shilling, what's that?" I asked.

"It's a commitment, only volunteers get it."

"Will I go abroad?"

"Definitely, if you choose one of these Regiments," and he pushed a list of names over to me.

"I know people who have been in the Army since 1940 and they haven't been anywhere," I said.

"That won't happen with this lot," he promised.

All the famous names were there; the Gloucesters, the Hampshires, the Fusiliers and the Oxfordshire and Buckinghamshire Light Infantry.

"What's different about the Light Infantry?"

"They march quicker than the others."

"That's for me."

After signing the papers, he opened a cash box and took out a shilling and said,

"If you don't need it you can always put it in the benevolence fund box."

"I'll keep it, there's a News Theatre around the corner, I'll spend it there."

The news was good for me, the war was still on and the Eighth Army was holding its own in North Africa. One week later I had a free travel warrant to report to

Colchester. I know now I was only cannon fodder but nobody could have talked me out of it. For the first time my father tried to, he had been in the infantry in 1914 and told me about the Somme, Ypres and the Western Front but he promised not to shop me to the authorities. At last I was getting somewhere after nearly two years of trying to get into a war everybody said would be over by Christmas.

Clockwise from top left: the 1939-45 Star, the Italian Star, the Victory Medal, the German Afrika Korps Medal, the Line of Duty Medal, the Africa Star, the American Purple Heart.

Chapter 2

Nobody tells us anything

In Colchester, I met up with hundreds of other lads all from the latest call up. When I let slip that I was a volunteer, I was regarded as a mental case.
"You joined this lot for a shilling! You must be mad," they cried.

We were put in a cavalry barracks, minus the horses and we slept over the stables. My first encounter with the quirks of army discipline came on the very first day. We had to fill a large sack with straw from the stables below. This was our mattress. I was down the cast iron stairs quick as a flash and started stuffing; the other lads followed me down the stairs. The Sergeant turned up and had a fit.
"That's the wrong straw. It says 'A Company' on the door and you are 'B Company'".
Nobody told us we were anything, let alone a Company, but I pressed on and tried to explain that it would be no problem because it was all the same straw and 'A' Company could get theirs from the next stable. We had gathered a crowd by now and the lads all stood around to watch the drama.
"How can it be the same straw you bloody idiot if it says 'A Company' on the door?"

After the war someone published a book called 'An Apple For The Sergeant'. It described the fracas between the Sergeant and I which followed in detail. I can only assume that the author was among the grinning crowd around the stable door. Anyway, the Sergeant won the day and I changed the straw. That was on day one; on day three, before we had uniforms, we were given duties in the barracks; mine was to scrub the broom handle just before the inspection. I wet the broom and put it back in the rack but the officer had seen this trick before.

"Put that man on a charge," he shouted and I spent three evenings in the cookhouse peeling spuds.

We were not allowed out of the barracks until we could walk upright and salute properly and that took about two weeks.

The main object of a training barracks is to change you from a thinking civilian to a person who does what he's told without thinking; if you don't buck the system you can do it in two weeks. For six weeks everyone shouts orders in your face and some of the guys were shattered by this transformation; this is not the same as being asked to do something nicely by mom. The first night in barracks I could hear people crying and one chap wouldn't take his clothes off to get into bed. The Sergeant sorted him and they took him away to some special camp; they had a cure for all types. For those who wanted to play it tough they were reminded that Colchester had a first class military prison, called 'The Glasshouse'. I was once part of the escort taking a prisoner there and can vouch that it is a very miserable place. On the other hand the Army tried to show how democratic it was, people would come round and say, "Anybody want to be an officer?" and a few ex-grammar school boys would put their hands up and they would be marched away, never to be seen again.

Very few memorable things happened in those early weeks but I'll mention one that did. At the end of the training period we had to mount a guard, a sort of poor man's Buckingham Palace show; civilians came to watch. On the great day I was there in the front rank facing the CO the Adjutant and some civilian personalities plus the Regimental Sergeant Major, all puffed up and ready to go. All old soldiers remember this from bayonet drill: when the order is given to 'fix', you don't fix but you withdraw the bayonet the full extent of the arm leaving a few inches in the scabbard.

On the order 'bayonet', you bring it round to the front and snap it on the rifle. Only mine didn't, it stuck: I gave it a final jerk. It flew out of my hand and slid across the parade ground where it came to rest at the feet of the RSM. What you should do at this point is nothing, but I forgot and nipped smartly out of the ranks and picked it up; the RSM was going purple, but he didn't move. I got back in the ranks, like nothing had happened; there was a long pause and then the changing of the Guard carried on.

At the end there was an inspection as the CO and one of the civilian dignitaries led an entourage of officers. When he got level with me, the CO whispered over his shoulder, "Take his name."
He didn't swear: the dignitary with him was a lady Councillor.
The next officer said, "What's your fucking name?"
I told him and the next one said, "You're in the shit son."
The one after him said, "You're in deep shit."
The last one was the RSM who said, "I have never seen anything like it in my life." Apparently there were a lot of things that he had never seen the like of in his life.

After the parade, I sat in the guardroom and waited for the onslaught; this was a serious breach which Hitler and Churchill would have to sort out. While I was sitting in the cell, several people came to look at me, although they didn't even lock the cell door; perhaps it wasn't treason after all. After a while the guard commander came in and said, "You're on next," and I went on guard again. It seemed that all was forgiven.

The next incident involved a guy in our barrack room named Turner who was a Birmingham lad, sloppy, slovenly and a mess but he was no trouble. We were only paid three shillings a day and most of us sent some home so nobody had money to spare. The highlight of our social activities was egg and chips for

9d [four pence] at a café in town. Turner used to join us but he never had quite enough money and always had to borrow a penny or tuppence. There's more about Turner later when I met up with him in action in Italy where he had even more serious problems, but his present situation was bad enough.

A soldier had molested a young girl and we all had to take part in an identity parade. Hundreds of us lined up and a little girl about 10 years old, with police and officials came along and had a look at us; it was a ridiculous situation, row after row of look-a-likes. There was no chance of picking anyone unless he had two heads, but way down the line there was a scuffle and she pointed out Turner. Two military policemen grabbed their victim and rushed him off at the double and we were dismissed. Back in the barracks we discussed it and all agreed there was no way it could be Turner. He never left the camp on his own and he didn't have the imagination of a set of mess tins. We tried to interest some of the officers but they said it was out of their hands. Later in the evening Turner came back to us, he was in a state but we calmed him down. Turner was one of life's losers and the incident was soon forgotten.

As the training period was nearly over we were given a number of limited choices like drivers, artillery, signals etc and when they asked who would like to be physical training instructors dozens of hands went up, including mine. I don't know how I fell for it but I had been a member of the Boys' Brigade gymnast team and was a very good athlete and I got carried away. Over forty men applied and the CO only wanted six so there had to be an eliminator. The CO was a simple soul and soon sorted it out; a fifteen mile cross-country run, the first six men in would do. I was in the first six. We were packed off to a special training school. As soon as we arrived you could see why PT was such a popular option; the camp was staffed by professional sportsmen, footballers, cricketers, golfers and even a fencing master.

This was a good way to sit out a war; nobody was going to be shooting at this lot. I realize there's a pecking order in life, but some people sit in the best seats all the time. I met Geoff Dyson who was one of the instructors; he became the Olympic coach at the first Olympic Games after the war. He said I showed some promise in the mile, who knows what would have happened if I had been listening.

Anyway, it was a good course and with such experts around we learned a lot; three of us passed out and returned to Colchester as Corporal PT Instructors.

Chapter 3

I am in charge

When you give stripes to a sixteen year old in a man's army there's bound to be trouble; I looked so young I couldn't even grow a moustache. I had to counter snide remarks with a threatening manner that ended in fights: I didn't come out too badly. I was pretty good at Judo and an arm lock would soon bring an apology. There were advantages too, nobody shouted in my face anymore and we didn't wear a uniform, just a striped jersey and blue slacks so we didn't have to salute all over the camp. Best of all, although we slept in the barracks with the men, we didn't have to make our beds up in that bullshit fashion, blankets folded, knife, fork, spoon and mess tins all in a straight line, so beloved by armies all over the world.

When the inspecting officer came round he would react in the usual fashion. "Whose is that bed there?" The Sergeant would reply, "PT staff, sir," and they would move on.
One could get used to all these privileges, no wonder everyone had put their hand up.

There was a Corporals' Mess and in the Mess hall we had our own tables served by foreign ATS girls. On the PT staff was Darkie Hobson who had been heavy weight boxing champion of India. He wasn't coloured but got his nickname because of his crinkly hair. He and I worked out a boxing routine for the new recruits. He would get into the ring and challenge everyone; there were no takers. Then I would appear, instant laughter; I was half his size. When I was in the ring Darkie would take a swing at me and miss. I would dive between his legs and kick him up the backside and run around the ring Charlie Chaplin fashion; what corn but with a captive audience laughter was guaranteed. Another staff member had been a circus clown and he showed me how to tumble and do a running somersault; I could impress the girls with that one.

There was also the opportunity to get even with the nasty types such as the Company office clerk. Although he was the same rank as me his office status gave him the opportunity to make trouble. Why he disliked me I don't know but whenever I turned up at the office with a group of men he would try to show me up in front of them. One day on pay parade he pulled me up for not coming to attention for the Pay Master. I was in my usual PT attire and didn't think it was necessary but the officer backed him up and made me go back and do it again.

When I bent over him to sign the book I whispered in his ear, "I'll get you, you bastard." He looked at me and smiled, maybe he thought in a punch up he would come off all right. We never had to square up to each other; the CO solved the problem for me.
He decided the camp staff were getting out of shape and everyone should do PT one day a week. We organised a 6am early morning parade so that it wouldn't interfere with the training periods. The CO said he would come himself and expected to be treated the same as everyone else in the ranks. One morning I came out to take my group and there was the Company office clerk.
"You are looking a bit flabby," I said, "we'll have to find you heavier pencils to push."
A few times round the field with a log on his shoulders and I had no more trouble with him.

As a schoolboy my nickname was Darlie and over the years it got changed to Dolly. It was still Dolly when I joined the Army. It stayed with me until one fatal day when I was in front of a squad jumping up and down; arm, shoulder, trunk and leg stuff. I could tell something was going on behind me by the look on the men's faces as they followed my example.

Then there was this cry, "Corporal, stand still."

It echoed around the gym. I turned and stood to attention. There was the RSM looking flushed as usual. He took his time and then he let rip; everyone got an earful.

"When you jump up, you come down without your hair. It's so bloody long you're like a bleeding Golliwog. Get it cut. I've never seen anything like it in my life."

He turned and marched away like a mechanical man; you could almost see the key sticking out of his back; but the damage was done and I was Golly from then on.

All NCOs were expected to charge squaddies with trivial misdemeanours. I didn't bother much with this rule. If I had charged everyone who threatened me, I would have been in and out of the Company office three times a day. There was though one occasion. We were doing PT in the rain and as we got wet one of the lads had hair so filthy it ran down his face like mud, so I booked him. There was no excuse for this kind of laziness but in a conscript Army you have a cross section of society. Some were trying to work their ticket but to prove you were so stupid the Army couldn't use you was very difficult. One lad wouldn't swing his left arm with his right leg; he would only swing two lefts or two rights together. It was more difficult to do it this way than the right way. We all tried but we couldn't keep it up, but he did and they took him away; we never found out if he got his ticket.

For someone like me who tried so hard to get into the Forces it was very strange behaviour. Although things were going well for me, I was never going to go abroad and I started to think about my original objective. What about the shooting war that's in all the papers day after day? There was even an invasion scare and everyone in Colchester had to go around armed with a rifle and five rounds of ammunition in their pocket all thc time. In the cinemas soldiers would be sitting staring at the screen with a rifle between their knees or sometimes between their girlfriends' knees. Taking your rifle with you to get your egg and chips in the local café sounds a bit farcical but there was a lot of tension and all of this made me think I was missing out on the real business.

My interest was renewed when the Paras came round on a recruiting drive. They set-up their equipment in the roof of the gym and showed the guys how to land, get out of the harness and various other techniques. There was nothing scary about it; I did some demonstrations to prove how easy it was but there were few volunteers. I put my name down but before the day was over the CO had me in his office.
"I'm not losing trained staff to a bunch of glamour boys. Is it because they get a red bonnet?"
"No sir, they get more money as well."
"So it's the money you want is it?"
"No sir. What I really want is to go abroad."
"If you had been with me at Dunkirk you wouldn't be so keen."
"I've got to find out for myself, sir."
"Well your request is refused. Go back to the gym."

I made other enquires and the Adjutant told me that the CO could not stop me from transferring to a Battalion. I was still in the Ox and Bucks Light Infantry (OBLI) and the 2nd Oxford and Bucks was an airborne unit so I made out an application. When I made my application to join the 2nd Battalion, I didn't know then that they would be the first troops to land in France on D-Day and be responsible for the capture of the famous Pegasus Bridge. Stephen E Ambrose wrote a brilliant book about this incident in the history of the 2nd Battalion. Nothing the 7th Battalion could do would ever match that but the 7th were about to go abroad and that suited me fine. The 2nd had to wait another two years for their moment of glory. I didn't know any of this at the time. Maybe the CO had interfered but I don't know, so minus my stripes, Private Golly arrived in Lincolnshire with mixed feelings. Had I done the right thing?

Missing stripes on a jacket are obvious and everyone wanted an explanation. I thought it was better to let the inquisitive think I had been busted, rather than let them know it had been my own choice. What with being underage, taking the King's shilling and losing a cushy job, I was already considered to be a weirdo. You only use the last three numbers of your army number and mine was 007. Imagine what else I would have had to put up with if James Bond had been around in the 1940s.

Chapter 4

Where to now?

The 7th Battalion had been training on the Yorkshire Moors and was in good shape; some of the lads had come from Colchester and remembered me. As an ex-NCO it took time to make friends but it all settled down. At least they didn't have an RSM who had never seen anything like it in his life.

The big question on camp was when were we off and where to? The desert campaign was doing very well and didn't seem to need any help. Then we were sent on fourteen days embarkation leave. I still couldn't understand why this seemed to worry some of them. New Street Station and the Military Police were everywhere, checking passes. There's an excitement around a railway station in wartime, packed with people in different uniforms and all nationalities. After I left the station and the MPs, I went into a toilet and sewed my stripes back on and my shoulder badge - it was two crossed swords and I liked it. I was only just seventeen and a bit of swank for the next two weeks wasn't going to do anyone any harm. Two weeks of drinking, dancing and bullshitting. I enjoyed myself but then it was over, stripes off and back to Lincolnshire.

Once back in the Battalion, we were issued with tropical kit; so it was the desert or Burma. Burma was the best guess; they didn't seem to be doing so well as the Middle East lot but our information only came from the BBC. Nobody else would tell us anything. Liverpool was the next move and on to a troopship, the Mauritania. I had only seen these big liners and all their luxury on films but it was impressive even though it had been striped down to house thousands of troops.

We marched up the gangway and down into the bowels of the ship. There was a Mess table for eighteen men and that was your space. We had to sleep under it, on it or sling a hammock above it but that was all the space you could have for eighteen men. Now an Infantryman soon learnt that he was at the bottom of the heap, that is until the guns begin to fire, then he got pride of place; but at the moment we were on a luxury liner and we knew our place: RN sailors, RAF, ATS and medical staff all above the water line, A and B decks reserved for officers. There was even a Guards Regiment and they were used to police the ship, to make sure the poor bloody infantry (PBI) stayed down below and out of trouble. When we had a lifeboat drill, I noticed the infantry had May West jackets, not the solid cork ones like everyone else. May West's were filled with kapok and only last a few hours in the water, if they can't get you by then, you're a waste of time and they are very cheap to make.

With the little free time we were allowed on deck I had a look around and discovered that apart from the crew, there were other nice little jobs on board that nobody ever tells you about in the recruiting office. There were PT instructors to give you PT in confined spaces, which was the name of the course they were on (nobody mentioned that one to me).

There were two guns, fore and aft, with a troop of Artillerymen. They also ran the Bingo, although it was called Housie Housie then. On a ship full of bored soldiers, Bingo was a money maker for the crew. The crew also ran wet and dry canteens; in the wet canteen they sold soft drinks, the dry for everything else. There was always a massive queue round the wet canteen so they sometimes needed help and if you could get in on it they would cut you in on the racket. You never poured out the whole of the bottle, there was always something left to sell to the next man. With a turnaround every few weeks of thousands of fresh troops, this must have been money in the bank. If you mentioned it to them, they would remind you there were torpedoes to worry about. We did have a U-Boat alarm on the third night but I still think they were on to a good thing.

The sleeping arrangements down below were unbelievably bad. There were air blowers but we were so crowded that they blew directly on to someone, so they were all switched off. The air was so foul it made people sick and as they struggled to get out, the Brigade of Guards made sure we stayed down. It was no good; we had to have a plan. A group of us got together to work out a diversion to get the Brigade off our backs.

By making a racket at one of the hatchways, a few of us got out of a second hatch and scattered around the ship for somewhere to hide. The lifeboats would be checked, they were obvious but I could see a pile of life rafts about twenty feet high which were for emergencies, clamped down in the centre of the deck. They were perfect if you could climb up without being seen. I took another guy into my confidence and told him to keep it quiet; we didn't want a mob in on this. We covered for each other and got on top. The rafts had a canvas centre and they sagged so you couldn't be seen from the side. We stayed up there for most of the night and made plans to get blankets and a water proof but we thought even if we get wet, we'll still be better off out of that stinking hold. If we were not seen getting up and down we could ride out the rest of the voyage like that. My buddy on the raft was Arthur Wood from Stoke-on-Trent and we became very close friends up until his unfortunate death in 1944. Arthur and I got very skilled at sneaking up onto the rafts after dark and off again before daybreak.

The rest of the guys in the hold were in very bad shape and at meal times nobody could eat so there was plenty for some; the food was very good and the fresh baked bread was excellent. There was a lot of seasickness and even I used to get sick but I never felt ill with it, just sick. In each of the groups of eighteen, two men were detailed to be the 'muckos', to fetch the food for our entire group from the galley. All of the muckos lined up every day and on one of those days I felt a bit strange and threw up all over the man in front of me. Quick as I could, I turned round to the next man and asked, "Who did that?" Nobody ever knew it was me because I didn't look ill so I got away with it.

For the whole trip we slept on the life rafts, which was fine until we docked in Algiers, North Africa in the middle of the night. When we climbed on the rafts we didn't notice a floodlight just above us, it wasn't switched on until we docked. Then every insect in Africa made straight for it, from giant ants to locusts, they covered the whole top of the raft and we were still asleep: but not for long. Sitting up with clouds of flies round our heads waving our arms frantically, we were being eaten alive and we panicked. They spotted us from the deck and ordered us down with shouts of, "Put them on a charge." Still brushing our clothes to get rid of the crawlies, we were marched down below. Down in the hold it was as bad as ever, so apart from a few bites we were still better off than they were.

If we had sailed a few months earlier we would have gone round the Cape of Good Hope and South Africa then up through the Suez Canal. A journey that long would have been unbearable, but the 8th Army, the Desert Rats, were doing such a good job that the Mediterranean was now accessible through the Straits of Gibraltar, so we took the short cut. Algiers, the first foreign county I had ever seen. At school we had a teacher who used to tell us about holidays in France but that was as near as kids like me got to the great beyond.

The next morning there was no hurry to disembark so we leaned over the rails to watch the unloading; it really was a culture shock. Down on the quay there were gangs of Arabs in groups of about a dozen with an overseer in a dirty white suit and a pith helmet, carrying a bamboo club, one end of which was loaded with lead. He would point to one of the nets swinging off the ship and they would run over to unload it; then someone threw down a cigarette and they broke ranks to go and get it. The overseer went mad and laid into them; we booed him and threw down more cigarettes, all the other gangs seeing there was a chance of getting some 'freemans', rushed over and joined in. It was chaos; the overseers used their clubs viciously and there was blood everywhere, it was like one of those Hollywood slave movies. Finally, we were ordered to stop messing about and get ready to disembark.

Chapter 5

Abroad at last

We marched through the town to a camp in the desert where we were guests of the French Foreign Legion. They were great. There was no Hollywood Beau Geste here but real soldiers. Apart from their cap, they were dressed the same as us in khaki and most of them had thick beards. We were with them for two weeks and every night they put on a show, usually a French farce, we couldn't understand a word but they were very funny.

Algiers was made famous by a film called 'The Kasbah', which is the old Arab quarter and we wanted to see it but before we could go into town we had to have the 'dos' and 'don'ts' lecture. The dos included brothels, French run and very clean, the don'ts meant keeping off the trams and buses or you would get covered in fleas. The Kasbah was something else: it rose steeply at the back of the town and the further you went into the quarter the more bizarre it became: to watch a huge, fat Arab woman having sexual intercourse with a donkey whilst you drank your coffee or to roll coins down a sloping table so that a woman could catch them in her vagina, was a first in anybody's education. It all came to an end though and we were off to war in cattle trucks.

Cattle trucks are a convenient way to move troops and well, it's better than marching. So in a fly blown station outside Algiers we all piled onboard. The train moved off in an easterly direction and if the destination was Libya, it was going to be a long haul. Sitting with our legs hanging out of the doorway of the carriage I was getting to know my new mate Arthur. I called him Woody; he was two years older than me and much more mature. He had been a cinema projectionist before joining up and knew a lot about old Hollywood films. He showed concern about the way the Arabs were treated; I suppose that made him a socialist. I didn't give a damn; that probably made me a Tory but I knew nothing of politics at the time. There is no doubt that what we had seen over the last two weeks had been a revelation and this is why I had tried so hard to get abroad in the first place but as the train gathered speed there was one more surprise.

A boy ran along the track shouting that the police were after him and he held a cloth in his hand, saying he had stolen some jewels. Our attention was riveted; he was putting it over in pidgin English and the problem was obvious, he needed to get rid of the evidence. I was interested immediately and my enthusiasm influenced Woody, who was nearest to the Arab thief.
"How much?" I shouted, fearful that I was going to miss out on a golden opportunity.
Give him some English money, I told Arthur and raked through my own pockets but there wasn't enough.
"Come on Woody, for God's sake give him some," and Arthur handed over his last few pounds and dog-eared ten shilling notes.

We grabbed the dirty bag of priceless gems. Well anybody can be clever after the event and we stared at the bits of broken glass, too late to do anything about it. The boy had timed the train speed well; we would have stuffed them down his throat if the train had suddenly stopped but there was no chance of that and the boy gave us a hearty wave; our lesson was over.

At a steady 15mph we chugged along the coast; it was a bore and the only relief was stopping for meals. It was during this period of boredom that I did something I have been ashamed of all my life. An Arab, sitting on his donkey on top of a sand dune watching the train go by, was about to have his life ruined by a thoughtless kid just seventeen years old. I had shot dozens of rabbits and hundreds of small birds but now I took aim at a man. I don't think anybody noticed what I'd done, but when they heard the shot they thought, "That's a good idea", and started potting off at anything: telegraph poles, goats, donkeys - but no Arabs; they had all got their heads down. When I fired at that man, all I knew for sure was that he fell off his donkey; it could have been surprise if the bullet had gone past his ear or he could have been wounded, but the moving train made sure I'd never be able to check. I've thought about this incident over the years and I hope that I missed. When I told Woody about it he was disgusted. I tried to jolly him up by saying he was probably a relation of the boy who cheated us at station but he was not amused.

We trawled on through Algeria, Tunisia and arrived in Libya. They put us in a tented camp in the middle of nowhere; Arab traders soon surrounded us and set up a market nearby. I had brought a small diary and decided to keep notes; I've still got it but most of the pages are missing and it finally fell to pieces. I shall refer to it wherever possible but there's nothing to report so far except sand and more sand. I left out the incident with the Arab as it could have got me into a lot of trouble.

Rations were mean and I was always hungry but there was plenty of bread so I solved the problem by buying some date jam in the market. Everyone who had been in the desert more than five minutes, told me that it was the wrong thing to do.
"Look at the flies," they said, but I was greedy and got stuck in.
I went down with the worst case of dysentery I have ever had in my life. I crawled to the Medical Officer's tent and an Italian POW, who was doing fatigues duty, came round and gave me a drink of water and helped me to stand up in front of the MO. The water I had just drunk ran down my legs like green slime. The MO

shouted at me and started to kick sand over the mess on his floor.

"Get outside and get on that jeep." He then gave orders for me to be taken to hospital. I think he thought he was in danger of catching something I was in such a state.

The hospital was American, just like the TV series that appeared in the 1970s called MASH, but I was dying and could not take in the good points. They purged me until I was hollow and slowly brought me back to solid food. I was the only 'limey' in there and got a lot of attention. A week later and feeling much better I realized how generous the Americans were. The Sergeant in the next bed was a professional card player in civvy street and he practiced all day long using a new deck of cards every few hours. In the British Army someone would have a dog-eared pack all screwed and battered and that would be it. I was going to be very popular when I handed out the Sergeant's leftovers. Just as I was ready for discharge I was stung by a large insect which I had trapped when I lay back on the bed and it made a mess of my shoulder, so I was in for a few more days of treatment; then I was ready to rejoin my Unit.

I was now in the 56th Division, with a Black Cat on my shoulder tabs and part of the American 5th Army. The Black Cat was never to become as famous as the Rat on the British 8th Army shoulders but we made our mark and soon the Cat signs were appearing everywhere. I learned that these men had come the long way round, before the Mediterranean was open and had already visited places like Cape Town, Bombay and Iraq; I had missed all that because I had agreed to become a PT instructor. I felt very humble mixing with those men; they had seen action fighting in the desert with the 8th Army and at a place called Enfindville they had suffered real casualties: my two weeks in hospital with dysentery didn't stack up very much against that. We still didn't know what they were going to do with us. The Arabs told us that we were going to invade Italy: so much for security.

We were in time for a visit by the King and as luck would have it, he inspected us. He had come out from England to do a bit of flag waving. The papers said, "The King visits the front line," well hardly but he did go to Malta; that was as near to the action as he got. During the inspection he passed about ten feet from me and I'm sure that he had makeup on but that was not unusual; amongst all our suntanned bodies he would have looked ridiculous.

While I had been away in hospital the CO had had an idea; he wasn't going to have his men squatting like wogs on the toilet. The Arabs, not wise to our unhygienic ways, preferred two platforms for the feet and a small hole between them; in this squat position, the body is not in contact with the seat. Many Europeans using them had accidents and scrubbing the heels of your boots in the washroom of a posh hotel was very embarrassing. The CO would have none of this, so he had ordered some Arab contractors to build some lavatories with proper toilet seats; it was nearing completion when I arrived. Army toilets, when on active service, are governed by rules to be as hygienic as possible. I'll tell you about some of the methods before I go back to the CO's state of the art contraption.

It was customary when setting up camp to detail two men, preferably defaulters, to construct the field toilets. If everyone had been behaving themselves then, "that man there," served the purpose just as well. The task was not difficult, simply find a secluded spot and dig a hole. The ingenuity of these men varied and the spot may well have been behind the Chaplin's tent or a quarter of a mile up the lane, but the true artist would choose a field of corn or tobacco where one could spend many happy hours meditating.

On one occasion during the Italian Campaign, I was sitting on a pole in the midst of a field of Indian corn; the tramp of many feet had worn a narrow path, but for all that it was isolated. As I sat there, looking at the corn cobs and wondering if they were going to be eaten by chickens or made into pipes, I heard a crashing sound. Whatever it was it was not using the path. A wild beast perhaps? I waited as it came nearer. I was right; it was a Sergeant in great haste probably caused by the local wine, smashing down the waist high corn, undoing his braces as he came. He jumped like an acrobat on to the pole which twanged and vibrated like a fiddle string. I held on grimly; the consequences of falling off were far more sever than those facing any man on a high trapeze; he would only land on sawdust.

When things had settled down, he turned to me and said, "That's the way to do it, no hanging about."

Not having the Sergeant's skill, I climbed gently off and made my way back down the track. When the camp broke up the hole was filled in and a stake, with an appropriately worded notice such as, "Soiled ground Feb. 1943," was placed in the centre. The reason for this was obvious, the Army bred single mindedness and the risk of digging in the same place twice was very great indeed.

As with all great ideas, one of them has to be a special and I met mine on an Infantry Landing Craft known as ILCs; it was a bit of maritime ingenuity. Landing craft were never meant for luxury cruises and the designers assumed that thirty or forty men could contain themselves for two or three hours without difficulty but the Salerno landings were not going according to plan and we had to lay off out at sea in a safe zone, for how long was anybody's guess. Consequently, we could have finished up to our ankles in shit and vomit, so the two Navy boys who were in charge of the boat made a 'thing' on the stern. Two long beams of wood were run out over the edge and a narrow plank was nailed across the far ends; there was no way of bolting the contraption to the boat so it was made secure by laying the anchor over the beams on the small piece of deck then a piece of rope was hung from the rigging for the victim to hold on to.

Throughout the day, 'sitting the plank' became the main entertainment for a group of bored soldiers. My stomach warned me not to laugh with the others as I had not been feeling too well and my dysentery was still giving me trouble. Sure enough in the middle of the night nature was insisting that I take the trip; at least I wouldn't have an audience: it was pitch black. I groped my way along the rail in the darkness took a firm hold on the rope and edged my backside along one of the wooden beams. 'Don't look down' was the secret. If there were any sharks in the Med they would have had no trouble digesting their dinner; that huge propeller would make mincemeat out of anyone who fell overboard. Bearing all these facts in mind, I reached the sitting position. It was like being on a seesaw; every time the stern went up the plank would rise in the air and the anchor would change its position. The vision of the anchor sliding right off the end and leaving me top heavy caused me to grasp the rope and twist it round and round my wrists. Never has it taken so long to do nature's bidding, it seemed like a lifetime before I could get back to the bottom of the boat.

The toilets I have described so far are the 'here today and gone tomorrow' type. For the semi-permanent camp a more elaborate construction was needed, which brings me back to our dear CO who was building an architectural masterpiece in Libya. At the opening ceremony, the sight that confronted us was unbelievable; it was about thirty feet long, brick built with canvas nailed to poles for privacy but the seats had been cast in concrete four feet square. The hole was the right shape but unless you were twelve feet tall it was impossible to sit down. Can you imagine twenty men going about their business, some standing, others squatting and some trying to sit with their legs straight out in front. In all that sun it was like sitting on a stove. We didn't have to put up with it for long; we were off to invade Italy; just like the Arabs said we would.

The Regimental insignia of the Oxfordshire and Buckinghamshire Light Infantry.

This is a story about the boys who became men in the first few minutes of hearing a burst of machine gun fire;

this is a story about the boys who never used their new manhood, because they never heard the second burst.

This is a story about the boys who never had a girl, no matter how much they boasted and now they never will.

This is a story about the boys who simply ran out of luck or cunning.

This is a book dedicated to all those boys whom we left behind in Italy – The D-Day Dodgers.

The cemetery at Monte Cassino and some of the D-Day Dodgers who we left behind.

Chapter 6

It's the real thing

Enough has been written about the invasion of Sicily and Italy and I don't want to repeat it here. The big picture is not available to the ordinary soldier and he is not aware that huge mistakes are being made at his expense. General Eisenhower made a speech about Italy surrendering; to the average squaddie this means the Country you are about to invade has packed it in so it's going to be easy. It was just the opposite; the Germans had moved all the Italian soldiers out of defensive positions and replaced them with their own battle-hardened troops from the desert campaign. The landing met with stiff resistance, especially the 56th and 46th Divisions. We were delayed and when we finally landed it was onto a false beach; we ran out of the boat into deep water. Equipment was dumped all over the place as we tried to keep our heads above the water; my dickey stomach was forgotten immediately and we lay on the beach gasping with Beach Masters screaming at us to get a move on.

Churchill referred to Italy as the soft under belly of Europe; I wish he could have seen this lot. British POWs were being forced to walk in front of German Tiger tanks as hostages whilst Heinz Guderian's Panzers were moving into position. In spite of all this a beachhead was established. This massive assault was completely overshadowed by the Second Front ten months later but nevertheless the lessons being learnt here at our expense saved the lives of hundreds of men on 6th June 1944 - D-Day.

Some interesting rumours began to circulate about mutiny and desertion from the beach and the cowards who had put us in more danger, if that was possible. It was completely untrue. The book written by Saul

49

David over fifty years later, explained how the men embarked from Tripoli thinking they were going home after their successful desert campaign. They thought they were going home to take part in the Second Front which was being demanded by Stalin. Instead they landed at Salerno to make up for our heavy casualties. They had been double-crossed by their commanders and they refused to join strange Units. We might have been more sympathetic if we had known the facts.

The Black Cats pushed inland and now I found out what a shooting war was all about; the next few months were very scary. At a place called Battipaglia, the Guderian Panzers stopped us dead in our tracks; it was the Fusiliers who bore the brunt of this attack. Being in action is not like the films portray it, lining soldiers up in your sights and popping them off. Your first encounter is usually artillery or aircraft fire. If you are dug in on a static front, you fire at bushes and shadows just to let the enemy know you are still on your toes but it's unlikely that any real damage is done. When the Panzers counter attacked at Battipaglia, all that changed. It was our first major set back; we were forced out and we had only been in the Country a few days.

The history books put it like this, "The British attack on Battipaglia was driven off." Just one line of information. Let me explain what this really meant, not a bird's eye view but a worms eye view. You are down below the ground in a two-man slit trench, the longer you are there the better the trench becomes. It's now deep enough so only your head is showing. Close friendships are being formed and you try to share your lot with people you like and trust. I was with Woody most of the time but my partner had gone off to do some chores so I was on my own. First the mortars rain down, then maybe small calibre fire and if it's a direct hit or very close, then that's it; you can only crouch at the bottom of the trench and hope.

Then the mortars stop and they start throwing hand grenades with plenty of machine gun fire. You can throw grenades back of course, but that means getting into a better position and showing yourself and that's what the snipers are waiting for. German snipers were a special breed; they were marksmen with extra skills in map reading and camouflage. We had snipers too but they were just good shots; not in the same class as Jerry. Jerry was a First World War word, we called them Teds after the Italian translation Tedeschi. I remember on a later occasion when a sniper had been giving us a lot of trouble with several kills to his credit, he decided to give himself up. He walked across the field towards us with his hands on his head grinning all over his face. A Sergeant picked up a Tommy gun and emptied a full magazine into his body, none of us thought this cavalier attitude was acceptable, but snipers were different, a breed apart from ordinary battlefield soldiers.

The German counter attack was terrifying. No training can be a substitute for the real thing and we did not have enough experience to deal with it. Those grenades they were throwing meant that they were only twenty yards away and going to rush us any second. Maybe inspired leadership would have saved the day, but inspired by whom. You are on your own, in the dark and you can hear the other guys making a run for it, only Errol Flynn would have stayed at his post under these conditions. I looked behind me into the blackness, scrambled out of the ground and ran like hell.

One of the lads couldn't get out of his trench quick enough, so he lay still at the bottom and prayed; a storm trooper stood over him with a Schmeisser machine pistol and sprayed the trench. He swept the gun round and not a single bullet touched the cringing squaddie, then the storm trooper ran on to the next trench and did the same thing. When we regrouped

51

later he told us all about it. After the German ran off he was worried about being taken prisoner. He had a lot of German loot and he thought they would knock him about when they found out, so he tried to get rid of it while lying still at the bottom of the trench. Even the belt holding up his trousers was German; his antics trying to get it off without moving were very funny but we didn't know whether to laugh.

Looting was something we were going to be very good at in due time, in our limited way of course, though officers with transport were in the best position. No infantryman could carry paintings around with him but a bottle or two of brandy was no problem.

After the Battipaglia shake up, we moved northwards much wiser men. It happened again at a place called Baronissi and we behaved exactly the same and a lot of men died. How some of us finished up in the ruins of Pompeii I can't say, I just tagged onto a Sergeant who had tagged on to some Guards who seemed to be on their way to Naples. When more of us showed up, there was even more confusion. There is nothing like being fired at to concentrate the mind; a group of us ran into some ruins though we didn't know until later that they were the famous Pompeii ruins.

Not only did we have the Germans to contend with but Italian kids as well. While we ran round the ruins trying to keep our heads down, these kids would try to sell you something. One nine year old was trying to sell me a badge, I was crouching behind a block of marble trying to be invisible and this kid was giving the game away. The badges he was selling were a novelty depicting a duck on the wing, neck out-stretched and wings beating but when you turned it upside down it was a man's penis and scrotum. I was not in the position to admire the artistic merit of the purchase only glad for him to go away. These kids were either absolutely fearless or plain stupid. In Naples the street urchins would pull some amusing stunts on our lads, they must have been the future Mafia.

The push for Naples was called off; the population had rioted so it was left to the Brigade of Guards to sort it out and we are off to cross a few rivers. The Guards eventually took Naples without any help from us and we got back into Baronissi a week later. Everyone wanted to know what we were doing in Pompeii; we didn't know, we were just following the man in front. It was thirty years before I went there again; it's a very interesting place when you have time to look around.

We were close enough to the coast for the Royal Navy in the Bay of Naples to use their guns, so now we could push North West with a lot more confidence. We kept being told that we had air supremacy, so what were all those Messerschmitt and Focke Wulfs doing flying around. Even the RAF didn't seem to have its act together; a Spitfire strafed us as we marched along the road. The bursts went between each man; if the pilot's angle of attack had been steeper he would have got every one of us. This problem was so serious it was suggested that we were issued with coloured scarves for identification. Unlike bomber pilots, fighter pilots never knew where they where, more to the point they didn't know where we where. The scarf idea was dropped; I suppose the Germans would have used them once they found out.

River crossings were the next big learning curve, though there were plenty of minor rivers and streams which we just waded across. The Yanks had been stopped at the Rapido River, so now we had to show them how it was done. We had to cross the Volturno in flood, with the Teds sitting on the opposite bank. We rehearsed on a quiet piece of water, away from the front line, using canvas boats and we didn't do it very well. It's not a pleasant thought, only canvas between you and a bullet and the collapsible boats kept collapsing; lessons were being learnt the hard way. Our first attempt to cross the Volturno was a complete failure; once the enemy lit us up with flares in the middle of the river it was an apocalypse, a stampede to get out of the light of the flares. We gave up and tried again further up the river, success this time, but we never used the canvas boats again. There were rumours that we might be taken out for a bit of a rest; we had been in action none stop for a month. It all came to nothing, though we did have a short break whilst we took on some reinforcements and our old friend Turner from Colchester was with them. We took it in turns to tell him horror stories. Those of us who were in at the start felt lucky and formed groups with people we could rely on. I can still remember some of their names, Daws, Palmer, Wright; those three in particular because I was with them when they died.

After the successful river crossing we were up in the mountains for so many months that I cannot remember the order in which they were taken: Camino, Croce, Monte Masico. We had our own names for these points on the map, such as Bare Arse Ridge where the Guards were hanging on for dear life: we took over but we were in just as much trouble. The whole campaign was grinding to a halt because of bad weather and casualties. During the stalemate we dug in and set up a routine. What is not generally known is that the Army had a rum ration sent up to the front every night with the compo rations. The Navy had rum every day wherever they were, but they were the Senior Service so we only got it when we were in trouble and that meant in action. Front line rations were the only thing I can recall that we had that was better than the Americans. Their KP rations were rubbish and included comics and chewing gum! The rum sent to us was always for a full Company and our platoon was always twenty or thirty percent under strength, so we had extras. We could get quite tipsy, which would account for our strange behaviour and strange it was. In the daytime, standing in your slit trench with orders to fire at anything that looked suspicious, gave you plenty of scope. There was a dead German about forty yards away, the helmet nearest to our position so all day everyone fired at the corpse. The bullets nibbled away at the body like maggots until it was reduced to a jelly.

The average foot slogging infantryman was a simple soul, he did what he was told and hoped for the best. A few days before, we had captured a place called Roccamonfina; it was all over the news but the name meant nothing to us. What was on every squaddie's mind was, are we going to get pulled out of the line for Christmas?

I was still trying to keep my diary topped up with information and it says something about a train journey south. I remember the train ride but we were stopped by damaged track and came back. What they had in mind for us we shall never know. Back at base, the only changes were that Moroccan and Indian troops had been brought in with the replacements that came to us and apart from Turner, there were some that fitted in and some that didn't. One of the latter was a German Jew. He was very useful because of the language but he made no effort to be one of us; he had his own agenda.

There was another guy I became very pally with, he was an American and I never found out if he was a phoney or not but it didn't matter, he was a Yank. Everywhere there were soldiers from the Commonwealth and they all had shoulder tabs but he was the only one with the word America on a British uniform. Not only that, he had a Texan drawl and a .45 automatic pistol on his hip; he was a mystery and great fun.

The Germans set up a series of defensive positions all the way north, The Barbarosa Line, The Gustav Line

and The Caesar Line. They were hard to break through and so we dug in facing them. It was more like 1914 trench warfare and each platoon had to take its turn on night patrols. We had a Company Commander who took this a stage further; his idea was for volunteers to form a platoon to do all the patrols so that they would become specialized at the task and as a carrot there would be no chores in the day. When the main attack went in the platoon would be in a reserve position; it sounded good to me so I volunteered. The keen young officer put in charge of the operation set up a tent and nailed a notice to a tree, 'Battle Patrol Headquarters'.
His only question to me when I went to see him was, "Can you swim?"
"Like a fish, sir."
"Good, you're in."
I tried to talk Woody into joining but he wasn't having any of it.
"When the Sergeant comes along to make you dig latrines," I said, "you say, 'sod off, I'm in Battle Patrol'."
It was no good though, he didn't believe in volunteering for anything.

The next few nights were very exciting times. It might be a small group of five with orders to grab a prisoner or a large group to shoot up some transport to make the enemy nervous. The Germans were doing the same thing and some nights we would pass each other in the dark and creep away without either of us causing any trouble. We had Thomson sub machine guns most of the time, the OBLI were never issued with the cheaper Sten gun; we looked like American gangsters. All that's left of my diary these days is a few pages in December 1943 but they record some of the events.

Dec 12 Jerry snipping from the village, one of the lads was killed, why don't we go and get him. (I must have been a pain in the arse for some of the section).

Dec 14 Today I killed a man, shot him in the guts only a few feet away.

I remember charging though a doorway firing a Tommy gun. The German was standing by some stairs. He went down and I ran over him and up the stairs. I ran from room to room firing like a madman. There is a strange compulsion, when the blood is up, to ignore self-preservation. I never saw anyone else in the building. When I had calmed down, I stood at the top of the landing looking at the dead German at the foot of the stairs; there was a Sergeant sitting by the body going through the pockets. I was enraged, I swung the gun round and screamed at him, "Leave him, he's mine." The Sergeant looked up at me and ran out of the building. I must have looked deranged. I walked down and sat by the body; my burst of fire had caught him in the midriff and I couldn't see his weapon, he may even have been unarmed. My Army Pay Book says I failed on the machine gun test but the targets were not as close as the one I was sitting beside.

Dec 15 Can't help thinking about yesterday; I wish he had been older.

What would a doctor have made of my state of mind? There was no doubt we were all changing, terrible things didn't seem so terrible anymore.

Dec 18 Can draw eight hundred Lire if we want it. With all the loot I'm getting, I don't need pay.

Dec 22 Section leader killed, they will be round to get someone to accept a stripe. We all agree not to accept.

I was always being asked about promotion. They knew I had been a Corporal in 1942 but I was one of the lads so I refused. I know that it was a mistake, but that kind of bonding could only happen in wartime.

It was nearly the end of the year and the previous month had been bad with plenty of setbacks. According to the News we were always winning, so why were we at a stand still in front of the Gustav Line, in the mud and going nowhere for Christmas? There was great pressure on at home to start a Second Front in Europe and a Member of Parliament called Lady Astor was making a noise, saying that we should be pulled out of Italy; she called us the D-Day Dodgers. None of us would have minded coming home to fight the war from Blighty but it's not up to the rank and file and we didn't like being called Dodgers. They made up a song for her; I'll use a verse whenever it's appropriate, (with apologies to Lili Marlene.)

We landed at Solerno, a holiday with pay,
Jerry brought his bands out to cheer us on our way,
Showed us the sights and gave us tea,
We all sang songs, the beer was free,
We are the D-Day Dodgers in sunny Italy.

Chapter 7

Go and see what's what.

The German counter attacks were just as violent as ever but we put up a better show and the stalemate continued. We were on the move at last; Christmas was over, not that anyone had noticed but it's the river this time and we are supposed to be good at getting over rivers. My father used to tell me about one Christmas on the Western Front in World War 1, when the front line declared an unofficial truce. In 1916, soldiers from both sides walked across 'no man's land' and shook hands. Perhaps in the Great War the soldiers had more compassion than we did because our Christmas came and went with no change.

The shells came flying over as usual but with a new twist: pamphlets. Whether this kind of propaganda was effective I don't know but I never saw anyone take them seriously. The pamphlet was about 6" x 4" and they varied from funny to sinister. One was a form which asked you to fill in your name, rank and number, hand it to any German NCO and you would be guaranteed safe conduct; your family would be informed immediately. Another, with a picture, showed a road with a line of British rifles stuck in the ground every few yards with a British helmet on the top of the butt. The caption said, "There are many roads to Rome, but none for you Tommy". The road was the Appian Way where the Romans had crucified 6,000 slaves after they had put down a rebellion in 71 BC. The history lesson was lost on most of the guys. Another pamphlet had an American soldier in England with a girl up against a tree and the punch line was,
"Where's your hubby, honey?"
"He's in Italy, in the mud."
This caused a few laughs.

The Gustav Line was a tough nut to crack and it caused the Generals to miss their morning coffee. The answer seemed to be to get over the Gariglione and all will be well; so off we all went to prepare. We had some practice with American flame-throwers, even though we were not issued with them and some instructions on German light machine guns. Unless we were going to join the Wehrmacht, this was what was known as 'R 'n' R' – rest and recreation. It was restful because we were not being shot at and recreational meant the odd game of cards between the pep talks, but we knew this was only the lull before the storm. We were all worrying about the river: we hoped it wouldn't be canvas boats again. We saw some DUKWs; they had used some of these on the beach landings; they kept your feet dry and there was plenty of armour plate; perhaps it would be a push over!

We dug in about two miles from the river. That night we got the order to move and could soon see the river; the orders for quiet didn't need to be given twice. We were going over on rafts. Although it sounds bad, the engineers had done a good job. They had cleared mines down to the river's edge and marked the paths with white tape. The rafts, which took about fifteen men crouched down, were slowly pulled across to the opposite bank. Once we were over we spread out into a defensive position. We came to realise that there were some people in front of the infantry with a difficult job to do. The engineers had done a fantastic job. How many rafts there were I don't know, but they had to get the whole Division across; that's thousands of men. We were first over and had no trouble, but we did not expect to get away with it completely and that night, there were casualties. I read somewhere that there were 186 casualties, which, as a percentage, is not bad for a Division. The German line was broken and we were up into the mountains again.

Mountain warfare didn't mean roping ourselves

together or wearing crampons on our boots; it was just different terrain. You couldn't dig yourself in of course, so for self-protection you relied on the rocks. Static positions for the machine guns would be piled round with broken rocks and these were called 'sangars'. There were lots of trails over the mountains and engagement with the enemy was a regular event. We knew how to be careful but we had just had a new Platoon Commander. Second Lieutenants didn't last long in this role; they were either killed in the first few weeks or they were moved up to Company Command and given a second pip on their shoulder. We would be back with our old Sergeant and that was best because he kept the risks down. Our new boss though was going to show us how it's got to be done. We were on some rugged terrain and facing a trail leading downhill and disappearing into the fold of the mountain.

"What's your name?" the officer said.
"Turner, sir." The gormless lad was standing in the wrong place. It could have been any one of us but Turner's bad luck made him the most likely.
"Go down there and see what's what," ordered the officer as he pointed down the trail.

We all looked at each other and thought, "See what's what?" That should give the lad plenty of scope. Turner ambled along with his rifle on his shoulder.
"For God's sake, look alive man," the officer shouted at the aimless soldier.

Turner dropped his rifle into the trail position and carried on. About fifty yards away he looked to his left, dropped his rifle to the ground and putting his hands into the air, walked out of sight forever.
The officer spun round on us and screeched, "Is he playing silly buggers or what?"
"That's Turner sir; he doesn't have enough imagination for subtle jokes," someone answered.
"So what's going on?" said our now puzzled leader.

"He must have seen something nasty, sir," was our best suggestion.

The officer took out his revolver and said, "Follow me."

He didn't need to tell us to look lively; we were well on our toes. This idiot could drop us in it if we were not careful. Down the path we went until we came to Turner's rifle. There was nothing to be seen but plenty of cover for anyone to keep out of sight. We made ourselves scarce whilst the officer strolled about asking questions. We could have made a book on him getting popped at any minute but he was lucky, nothing happened. We never saw Turner again. Was he now a POW or missing in action or simply loafing around in some Italian villa? Well, good luck to him wherever he is, we thought.

As a postscript to this story I did, only two years ago, find out what happened to the luckless Turner as I stood in front of his gravestone. Whatever events followed his capture, he somehow turned up again and was part of the Anzio landings. He died on the beach there, once more invading a country he had already invaded before. What a mess.

In these same mountains we were a small part of a much larger plan to keep the pressure on the Gustav Line and harassing tactics by small groups of the enemy was their way of slowing us down. The loss of Turner was sad because he was one of the original group but it made us use caution and we still had this new officer to contend with. He was the reason for my baptism of fire; my wound was not that serious but the whole experience was unforgettable. We were held up by a lone German with a Spandau machine gun. He was well protected by a sangar of rocks; we couldn't get near enough to use grenades and we had nothing else for back up. As we crouched out of sight behind a ridge the officer explained his plan,

"Right, we all spread out and go together on my call; before he gets over the surprise we will be on him."

This chap was not going to make staff rank but his career was not my problem, so I figured that if I had to do something this foolish then don't hang about; do it fast and furious. Wrong. My bad judgment put me ahead of the others and Ted swung his gun round and concentrated on me. I could see him clearly and he had his mouth wide open. The only cover which lay between us were some loose boulders and I dived for one. It wasn't big enough but I had to get my head behind something. The burst of fire hit the rock before it hit my right leg. I was down but the hair-brained stunt worked because Woody, who was just behind me, ran forward, jumped on top of the sangar and fired down at the crouching German below his feet. He missed the man's head but the bullet went down the side of his neck. The exit wound was in his backside; the bullet must have passed through every vital organ in his body and death would have been instantaneous. I know all this because Woody came back to tell me all the gory details. My leg was a mess and we put a shell dressing on it to stop the bleeding.

The officer came over to me and was clearly pleased with himself,
"You'll be all right, the stretcher bearers will be here before long."
They all moved on to do their part in the bigger plan. It was a nice day; there was no rain for the first time in days so I just lay there; my leg was numb, no pain; I slipped from consciousness.

I can't be sure if I had actually been asleep. I was very weary and I felt strange although the loss of blood could account for that. I had no idea of time and it was still very noisy. We were only a small part of the big plan and the artillery had moved on but I can't imagine sleeping through all that racket. Below the barrage of noise there was stillness at ground level; barren rock, loose boulders and polished surfaces but empty of life. I felt weird, there was no reason why I shouldn't be after all I'd been through but something was different. What was I doing here, I thought. I'll be eighteen in a few months time and after that I can't get out, not that I had ever tried. Back in 1940 I wanted to get into the shooting war and it couldn't get anymore shooting than this. I was wrong again. Suddenly I heard something and my daydream stopped immediately. The strange noise was behind me and it was difficult for me to move. I turned my head as far as I could and saw a Kraut crawling towards me. I pointed my rifle at him and he sat up on his knees.

"Nicht, nicht. Schiessen," he said with his hands in the air.

I had no intention of shooting him but I waved my rifle at him to indicate that I wanted him to come round to my front. When we came face to face I could see that he too was wounded. He was terrified; he stared at me and indicated that he wished to go down to our lines for medical attention. I wasn't ready for that yet so I made him get off his knees and sit; the kneeling position gave him too much advantage if he decided to jump me. This sort of confrontation must happen on battlefields all over the world; you're faced with the enemy and a language problem.

"You, prisoner." He understood that all right.

"Ya, ya," and his hands shot up again.

We compared our injuries but he wouldn't relax and kept staring at me. Well, if we can't be friends to hell with it. I poked my rifle in his chest and told him to turn out his pockets. He couldn't do it quickly enough; out came his pay book and some Italian money. Italian bank notes were big and decorative and as the Germans had been allies for years, the money was left alone but when we occupied the area we issued our special money which looked like raffle tickets; after that theirs had no value. I wasn't doing very well out of my prisoner but when he was pulling at his breast pocket I noticed a flash of colour round his neck and I wanted to see what it was. It was a medal which was only ever issued to the Africa Korps and I demanded that he hand it over.

I thought he would make trouble when I pinched his medal but no, all he wanted was to get away from me. He made some strange gestures and pointed at my rifle, from which I gathered that he wanted to use it as a crutch. I couldn't go along with that but I could see an iron picket not far away. They are used with barbed wire and what it was doing here God only knew. It couldn't be screwed into the ground so I suppose somebody realized he was carrying useless equipment and threw it away. I pointed at it and indicated to Fritz he could use it. He hesitated, staring at my gun; he really believed I was going to shoot him in the back. With a lot of arm waving and a few smiles I convinced him to try and off he went. He finally got to the picket and using it as a prop he gave me a wave and hobbled out of sight. I sat there looking at the pay book and the money; the medal was nothing more than a souvenir at the time but later in life it was very significant and the cause of a great disappointment.

The feeling in my leg was starting to get painful and as I started to think about sorting myself out, I heard English voices. It was such a relief but the first group of squaddies just stood around and stared at me as if I was a freak.
"What about a stretcher then?" I said.
The fact that I could speak jolted them into action. Yes, the medics were on the lower slopes but there were heavy casualties from the mortar fire. It appeared that we had got off lightly on the high ground. Just then, two stretcher-bearers appeared with a German soldier on the stretcher. One of the squaddies called them over. They took one look at me and whispered,

"Christ," and with that remark they tipped the German off the stretcher without ceremony: I was glad to see though that it wasn't Fritz, my earlier companion. In complete contrast to the treatment of their former patient, who was now lying on the ground moaning, I was treated with kid gloves.

"Careful, careful, don't shake him up," said one.

Only half an hour before I was contemplating getting down the mountain using the rifle as a crutch: this was royal treatment indeed. Finally, I arrived at an American Advanced Dressing Station. I was placed on the floor of the tent, still on the stretcher. My first thought was that nobody was going to pinch my loot and I stayed fully conscious and watched them.

The first one over was the Padre.

"Oh my God, look at this one. He's so young." I had nothing to add to his remarks and he went on, "I'll get the doctor right away."

The doctor knelt down by the stretcher and said, "Let's try and get the helmet off first."

He gently removed my tin hat and put it behind my head and after further examination he kept feeling round my scalp.

"There's no bleeding," he said.

"There's plenty of bleeding from my leg." I remarked, but he didn't even look round.

"We'll deal with that later," and carried on with his examination of my head.

"Don't you feel anything?"

"Only in my leg."

"Can you see clearly?"

"Yes."

The puzzled doctor reached for my helmet and held it up in front of me. I had a real shock at what I saw and it was unbelievable that I had no knowledge of this. The helmet was ripped open and the metal was rolled back like a sardine tin. Now I could see what all the fuss was about. No wonder Fritz was terrified, he must have thought I had massive brain damage; and that is why those squaddies couldn't believe their eyes either. My leg was ignored while the doctor took the helmet around the tent showing it to all his colleagues. People came over to see me and to confirm that my head was still on. How did it happen? When did it happen?

I know that it didn't happen in that first burst of machine gun fire or else Woody would have told me when he came back to tell me the gory details of how he killed the Ted but it was certainly before the German Fritz, had kept me company: so it will remain a mystery. I can only conclude that it must have been caused by shrapnel but it gave me a very close shave. I cannot recall everything which happened on that mountain top as I slipped in and out of consciousness but I don't think I had a peaceful sleep! I know of only one other case when a bullet went through an American helmet and went round and round inside, badly burning the top of the soldier's head, but there was only a small access hole in that case, not like the damage my helmet had suffered. Whatever the reason, I had an amazing escape. I never saw the helmet again; it's probably in some small American town museum or amongst the memorabilia of a non-combatant orderly.

First Aid stations near the front are different from other medical centres because their function is to stop the pain, cut down the risk of infection, tidy you up and pass you on. Some of the guys in the tent were completely out of it and just lay there, others like the walking wounded, came in quite cheerfully and sobered up as soon as they took a look around; there by the Grace of God and so on. An officer, who had been our Platoon Commander before he was promoted, came in, recognized me and said,
"It's Darlington, isn't it? Where are you hit?"

"In the leg, sir."

"Aren't you lucky. Look at me?"

He turned round to show a nasty wound in his backside.

"How am I going to explain this in the Mess?"

I remembered this officer when he took command of the Platoon, a bit toffee nosed but he was ok. He had a batman who took the mickey out of him. He used to say, "He tried to put some jam on his bread this morning and got it all over himself." I remembered this officer for better reasons though. We had been on several sorties together and he used to lead from the front, swinging his walking stick and shouting at the top of his voice in German. He may have been no good at catering but he was a very brave man.

"Come on Darlington, any suggestions?"

"You could say you were jumped from behind by an SS storm trooper with a knife."

"Come on man, I'm serious."

"Ok, sir. It was shrapnel; it goes in all directions."

"That's better. I can't have them thinking I was running away."

As I mentioned before, Second Lieutenants didn't last long in a Platoon, they either died or they were promoted. This officer was far better than the one I had been with a few hours ago.

The next day, the soldiers who had died in the night were carried out of the tent without any ceremony and I was told that I was off to Naples, which was now a very peaceful place with a big lovely hospital. Apparently, in peacetime the hospital in Naples was quite famous. I don't know what its Italian name was but for military purposes it was known as the 93rd General. The surgeon who treated my leg came to see me after the operation; he opened his hand and dropped a pile of metal objects on my locker, there were nine pieces. Only two were recognizable as bullets, the rest were just broken lumps of lead. The doctor explained that there was still a lot of stone grit in there but that it was impracticable to try to remove it, nevertheless it would work its way out in its own time, and it did; for many years afterwards little blue marks would appear beneath the skin and I would get them out with a needle like removing a splinter.

The doctor said that my wound was not serious and I was 'a lucky son of a bitch' and off he went to deal with more serious cases. I put the nine souvenirs with the rest of my loot and considered the possibility of doing a bit of selling in the hospital when I was up and about. Being up and about in a military hospital meant you had to work and I soon made myself useful. My wound was known as a 'Blighty one', but unfortunately, being so far from home I could not be sent back to Britain for treatment. If it had happened in France, within a few hours I would have been in an English hospital with all the family around the bed; well not my family but you know what I mean.

Self-inflicted wounds (SIWs) were common but if you were caught it meant a court martial. On my tour of duty around the wards I saw some of the patients handcuffed to the bed with the letters SIW boldly on display. The Americans even regarded syphilis as a self-inflicted wound and there were MPs in the wards taking names. There were a number of Navy casualties with horrific burns and scores of amputees. Amongst all this suffering you would not think there could be any humour in a place like that, but there was. A Corporal with one leg was teaching a Gurkha with no arms, dirty nursery rhymes in English so that he could recite them to the ward Sister, which he did with a great big smile. This little guy from Nepal couldn't do enough for memsahib. All this made me realise that by comparison I had nothing wrong with me and could expect an early discharge. There was talk of convalescence on the

Isle of Capri but it didn't happen and I was sent to a transit camp to wait my return to the Front.

The camp wasn't far from Naples and everybody in there was trying to stay there, not because of the fleshpots just up the road but to avoid the dreaded journey to the front line. Woody turned up one morning; he had been on my tail through the hospital. Neither of us were aware of the other's presence in the hospital. He had been struck by a motorcyclist. The Dispatch Rider's Sten gun had gone off when it hit the road and the bullets had shattered the 'Don R's' knee but Woody got away with a damaged shoulder and was sent to the 93rd. He was so pleased to see me but the prospect of going back up the line was not a happy one.
"Hello Golly. What's the score?"
"This place is a shambles but we'll soon work something out", I said.

It was only at meal times that there was any kind of order and that is when the NCOs took your name for the transport list. I had already sussed which of the NCOs didn't bother to check your name against your pay book, so a wrong name gave you a few days grace. Woody still had his loot and so had I, so we raised some cash and went to Naples to eat. It was a question of spoiling the pattern so that the camp staff didn't get used to seeing you.

Arthur and I had some great times in Naples but we knew it that couldn't last and sure enough a conscientious Corporal made it his business to check us out. We owned up to all the Charges and they made the usual threats about what they were going to do to us but we gave them that insubordinate smile that said we knew that nothing they could do to us would compare with where we were going. So we climbed on board the three ton truck and set off to see how the Gustav Line had managed without us.

Chapter 8

Russians and Generals

When Woody and I arrived at Battalion they were resting a few miles behind the line but our luck was out because the rest period was nearly over and there was a buzz on. The whole Division was going to Anzio. Whilst I had been in hospital I heard about the landing further up the coast but it was a pushover; everyone just walked ashore. It had been code named Operation Shingle. This couldn't be anything to do with us, could it? Someone soon sorted it out, Anzio was just down the road from Rome: the eternal city and home of the Pope.

"You and Woody had a good time in Naples, wait till we get into Rome."
The lads agreed, "Just because you had a bit of a scratch."
I wouldn't have put it quite like that, Woody still could not use a rifle properly because of his shoulder and I still had a limp but the lads were adamant, a good time was on its way for all.

What we didn't know was that Operation Shingle had turned into a shambles because of an incompetent General who had lost the advantage of surprise and now there were nine German Divisions trying to throw the brave lads into the sea. We were transported to Naples and put onboard Tank Landing Craft [TLCs]. Still not sure what we were in for, we made the best of it, mixed with the American tank men and had quite a few laughs over the next forty hours. I swapped my boots with a yank; how I convinced him British was best I don't know but a lot of the Yank drivers were coloured troops and only used as ferry men. At the time coloured men could not be used in combat; this attitude changed towards the end of the war. Palmer and Daws tried to out do each other swapping bits of uniform with the Yanks; we all looked a sight and we didn't care; we spent the night in good sprits.

By daybreak there was a lot of German aircraft about, more than we had seen in the south. It was now the 7th of February and the landing had taken place on the 22nd of January: what the hell had happened in the last sixteen days? Rapid briefings followed with officers trying to put a brave face on it. General JP Lucas was in charge: the Yanks called him Corn Cob Charlie because of his southern manner and pipe. This had become a battle of personalities. The obvious man for the job was General 'blood and guts' Patton but he was out of favour because he slapped a GI who was complaining of shell shock, so we were stuck with Charlie. Obviously we know nothing about all this, all we had was our own officers who were doing their best. A staff officer, no less, gave us the bad news,
"The British 1st Division is in serious trouble and a Ranger Battalion has been wiped out to the last man."
This was very bad news because the American Rangers are tough guys.

There's a place called the Factory and every Anzio veteran will know the name. It was a building that had changed hands several times between the Teds and us. The radio reports said that it was every man for himself.
"I thought we were going straight to Rome, sir?" a nervous voice asked.
"Rome! No chance. You'll be lucky to get back to the beach."
We lined up on the dock in our mixed up uniforms but none of the brass noticed what a mess we looked. We were off to the Factory about twenty miles away. On most offensives we got tuned in before the attack, but this was a rush job.

Anzio is now a legend, subject to numerous books and even a film, which I didn't consider to be very good. According to Hollywood, the British weren't even there. Names like The Flyover, Dead End Road, The Bowling Ally and The Lobster Claw have all been used to satisfy military gurus, but to our Platoon it was a war of little battles and skirmishes, none of which would make the history books but to us it was apocalypse every time. The Anzio offensive was supposed to bring about the capture of Rome and to link up with the main American 5th Army, bringing a quick conclusion, but it didn't work out. The General in charge had had a bad time at Salerno and he couldn't believe how easy this landing was. He delayed moving off the beachhead and gave the Germans time to consolidate their forces.

The German commander was General von Kesselring and he was very good at this kind of operation. It was acknowledged as one of the smartest moves in the Italian campaign. It was a stand off and we were being rushed up to fill in the gaps. I don't know about gaps, the Factory was a gapping great hole. We were in trouble before we even got there; my Company entered a deep wooded valley, the Germans were on the other side. The further down the valley we went, the closer we got to each other. It was decided to hold off until dark then select a good defensive position and dig in. Daws and I were one and two on the Bren gun. When darkness came, Daws and I crept down the sloping ground, found a spot and started to dig in. The weather was bad and getting worse. I could hear Palmer near by, someone told him to, "Shut-up, we don't know how close the bastards are." During the night, one man from each slit trench had to go and meet the quartermaster and collect the food and rum ration. Daws volunteered; I stayed in the trench which by now had a foot of water in the bottom. All the men returned but no Daws. I slid over to the next slitter to enquire if anyone knew anything.

"He had a bad time at Battipaglia remember," said Palmer.

Of course I knew that Daws was the one that had got stuck in the trench when the Kraut bullets had missed him by inches, but afterwards he made light of it so I didn't think that that was the trouble. I went back to my hole and spent the night on my own. When daybreak came there was still no Daws. There was no chance he could join me now; concealment was the game, no moving about. I spent the early hours peering over the trench with the gun well camouflaged in greenery. Suddenly there was a movement to my front; my sodden boots and freezing limbs were instantly forgotten. It was a German foraging about; he had no tunic on and he was right in my sights. I waited until he stepped into a large bush, slipped the bracers from his shoulders and swatted down out of sight. It was obvious what he was doing but my sights were still on the bush.

If Daws had been with me, we may have discussed the situation but on my own, wet and freezing cold with no food or rum ration, I was not feeling generous. I emptied half a magazine into the bush; there was a yell and then silence. I knew what was going to happen next after giving my position away, the whole side of the valley opened up. I crouched at the bottom of the trench in water and waited.

As soon as there was a lull in the firing I ventured to raise my head. The Bren was still on top of the trench where some bullets had struck it. I pulled it down for inspection. A bullet had hit the breach so it was impossible to cock it, which made it useless. I shouted across to tell Palmer. There was no sympathy from him.
"It's all your fault, you started all this, you trigger happy pratt." I sat down in the water trying to make the best of the situation.

The one good thing was neither side was going to rush the other. The valley was too steep for that kind of tactic but random shooting went on all day. It was a relief that no mortars had been set up but it was a long day waiting for the light to fade. When it was dark enough, people started to crawl about and Daws turned up.

I was very glad to see him but angry, "Where the bloody hell have you been, I'm starving."

He explained that the Quartermaster Sergeant had got him to help with all the rations. I knew the QMS didn't like coming up to the Front and tried to meet you as far back as possible then clear off leaving you to distribute the rations to all sections. Daws got lumbered and had no time to get back to me.

"Well, have you got anything to eat," I said.

"No, but I've got a water bottle full of rum." That's handy I thought, we'll keep it for ourselves.

"I'll go for the rations tonight. The Bren's no good. I can drop that problem on the QMS and give him something to worry about. He'll have to get another one and bring it up to us. I shot a Ted this morning, over there in those bushes. He was having a crap. He's still there. Nobody has been down to sort it."

Daws remarked, "I hope they don't. With one rifle between us we won't be much good."

He also said he didn't think we would be here another night; an officer would be round later with some orders. When the officer did come, the first thing he did was give us a bollocking.

"What's the good of that slit trench? It's too deep, you silly sods."

He was quite right of course. With nothing to do all day, I had been bailing out water with a steel helmet. Every time I scooped it up, I gathered mud. After several hours it had got deeper and deeper, but he was in no mood for excuses. He was nearly as wet as I was; it had been raining for days.

"I would make you dig another one but we're moving out in half an hour."

When the call came, we had a good swig of rum and followed the others back up the valley.

The most dangerous place to be at Anzio was the harbour. It was subjected to continuous shelling by the Germans. They were using a large gun nick-named Anzio Annie. A cruiser and a hospital ship had been sunk already. We on the other hand, were outside the perimeter and safe from the heavy stuff. There were no lines between the enemy and ourselves but we had to watch for machine guns in every building and barn.

There was not much rest under those circumstances; we had to be alert at all times, but when we did get a break a rather unusual event took place. There were about twenty of us loafing about in a barn; the Sergeant got worried about security and ordered me and another man to go outside and keep watch. We weren't very pleased but we went out and walked in opposite directions around the building. My colleague disappeared around the corner but I was only a few yards from the door when I saw the bushes move. Unconcerned I said, "Who's there?"

As the German soldier stood up he gave me the shock of my life, not because he was German but because of his size. There were big Australians and Canadians and even bigger Canadian MPs but this guy topped them all by inches. I pointed my riffle at his face, a single bullet in his huge bulk would not have stopped him and I wasn't going to let those hands that were above his head, like two sides of beef, anywhere near me.
He said, "Non Tedeschi. Ruskie, Ruskie".
I thought Russia was on our side and I didn't know at that time that when Germany first invaded Russia, Stalin was giving his county such a hard time that some of the peasants were glad to join the German Army. Later the Germans behaved so badly that they

lost their advantage and the whole of Russia was united against them.

How my Ruskie fitted into history I don't know but my immediate problem was, what to do with him. I pointed and he stepped onto the path. As I gestured for him to walk ahead of me towards the door, my colleague came round the corner and stopped dead in his tracks.
"Christ, don't let him get near you."
"We're OK," I replied. I looked at the Ted and said, "Ruskie, Ruskie."
"Ya, ya", he said with his great ham fists still in the air.
I asked my mate to go through the door first and watch him. "I don't fancy him grabbing me as I come through." Finally, we were all inside and then there was a commotion.
"Where the bloody hell's he come from", said one.
"He's Russian," I said.
"How can he be Russian, he's a German Para," said another.
"A parachute wouldn't hold him," said some wit.
"Whatever he is, go and tell somebody so I can get rid of him." My Teutonic giant kept saying "Ruskie, Ruskie" and I was glad when the MPs came and took him away.

I was the centre of attraction now and made the most of it by starting off and telling them the best way to run a war. The squaddies looked at me in bored amusement but I went on about how the powers that be were hopeless and couldn't run a chip shop let alone a war. All of a sudden they sat up and paid attention. "That's better," I thought and went deeper into my favourite subject, taking the piss out of authority. There was a tap on my shoulder and an officer's cane came into view. I turned around and all I could see was red. American Generals wear their tin hats but British Generals never do. Plenty of red

around the cap but there's no mistaking the rank. He gave me a little push in the chest with his swagger stick and said,
"If you'll go over there, sit down and shut up, I'll tell you about some of the problems we have at HQ."

I staggered over to a pile of straw and flopped down. I didn't hear a word of what he said; my mind was trying to remember if I had mentioned any names when I was addressing the troops. After a short speech he walked out followed by his aide-de-camp, who turned to me and said,
"You're already in the shit son, so keep it shut."

Nobody in the barn knew who the General was, he didn't introduce himself, but over the years I think I've worked it out. When General Templer took over the 56th Division he was asked about the Black Cat sign and it was reported that he said, "When the tail is pointing to the left, we attack on the left flank, when the tail is pointing to the right, we attack on the right flank."
"What if it's pointing straight up," a cheeky reporter had said.
"In that case we go straight up the enemy's arse."
Yes, I think our General was the type who could have said something like that.

The campaign was still going badly, the Factory was retaken by the Krauts and our casualties were mounting. Some reinforcements came to make up our numbers. One I remember was a military policeman. What he was being punished for we never found out, but all his brass was shining and his webbing was white so we told him to get it blacked up or he wouldn't last five minutes. Even though he took our advice he was still killed the next day. Other reinforcements included deserters who were given the choice of having their sentence dropped if they agreed to go back in the line. The authorities thought that being a beachhead they couldn't run away, if this included the Salerno boys, it still wasn't fair. It was only later that we heard that British casualties alone were over ten thousand.

It was still going badly for the whole campaign. The OBLI had their share and the Factory, which we were supposed to have sorted, was retaken. As February dragged into March we were looking very rough, never being able to dry out was the bugbear. When a Spitfire zoomed overhead to strafe some Germans up ahead, we envied the pilot with dry boots and clean shirt. Sometimes the plane would come screaming back with a Messerschmitt on his tail blasting away but that's nothing, dry clothes are the thing, bullets you take in your stride.

The Anzio campaign was fierce and it was a sad day for me when Daws was killed. We had been together on the Bren gun since we landed. On this unfortunate day we entered a collection of farm buildings, we were at Company strength and we were the lead Platoon. The firing took us by surprise and we dropped the Bren as we dashed for cover in one of the buildings. I say we because I don't remember who was acting as number one at that time.

An officer came in and said, "Get the Bren set up. I think the fire came from those hay-stacks."
He ran off before we could explain. He came back a few minutes later and saw that we still hadn't done anything.
"Get set up. What are you playing at?"
We pointed to the gun out in the open.
"Well go and get it then." The officer was getting annoyed.

Near the gun was a shallow crater, probably made by a small mortar bomb. I said I'd go first, grab the gun and set it up in the hole. With Daws still watching me I made a run for it. The fire that came down was too late; I was already in the crater with the gun. The hole was deeper than it looked and I set the Bren up in a well protected position. I couldn't tell where the firing came from but I blasted away at the haystack and was soon calling for more magazines. It was going to be harder for Daws to get to me because the Teds had a bead on me. The officer called out to tell me that he was going to work his way round and try to set the haystack on fire with a Verey Light Pistol. He was successful and as the fire caught hold Germans ran out from behind the stack. It was easy for me then and I shot several down but I needed more ammo. Daws made a run to me with the ammunition but he was hit. He landed by me in the pit with three gas mask containers full of magazines. He had a wound in his side but it wasn't too bad. He wanted to run back but I said wait. It wasn't just the haystack; there were a lot of other buildings around the area that could still give us trouble. I shouted to the other guys in the building to keep watch while I sprayed every likely place. The rest of the company was putting down some heavy fire and Daws decided to make a move. There was a lot of blood on his jacket.

"I'm going to get this fixed up", he said and made a run.

He didn't get eight feet before a machine gun burst caught him straight in the body. I blasted away at everything but to no avail; Daws' executioner had got away with it. I thought he was dead, but he died later in hospital.

We mustered for one last throw, everyone in the Battalion was involved; Company cooks who hadn't seen their rifles in years, clerks and storekeepers all had to turn out. We heard that Hitler himself had said that Anzio must be retaken and the German forces on the ground did their best to comply. Between the railway lines and the canal we put on a brave show but we had no strength and most of the time we were on the run. Finally, the 5th Division relieved us.

These boys had been in the Cassino area and if they had been told the same bullshit as we were, probably thought that they were in for a picnic, but one look at the state that we were in would soon convince them otherwise.

There were some delays before we could get a boat and we stayed around the Harbour, which was still being shelled by Annie but there were some compensations. The Yanks had set up a cinema show and you could listen to Axis Sally's sexy voice; Sally was always telling us to give up. We didn't have the luxury of going to the pictures or listening to the radio where we had been, so it was all very new to us.

Before we embarked the QMS and his boss, a particularly nasty Lieutenant, were trying to get rid of stock. They were standing in the back of a three ton truck shouting for us to fetch new uniforms and boots. The officer held up a pair and I said,
"I think I take a number eight, sir."
The officer raved at me, "You only think you take eight do you."

There was no need for the tirade that followed but I think he was still unnerved from the day before when he saw his first bit of action. It was obvious what was going on; they didn't want to be bothered with the stock when we disembarked. Well, we could all play that game. On the way down the coast we threw most of our equipment over the side. It was less trouble than cleaning it. My remarks about my boots were not stupid after all; my feet were in such a bad way I couldn't get them on, so over the side they went:
"Lost in action, sir."

Palermo and Cassino were taken in our stride,
We didn't go to fight there, we just went for the ride,
Anzio and Sangars were just names,
We only went to look for dames,
We are the D-Day Dodgers, in sunny Italy.

81

Chapter 9

Having a Lousy Time

We landed at Naples and they rushed us off to a delousing centre about twenty miles away. This was the British Army at its best; a good comedian could have lived off this stuff for the rest of his life. Lice were the bane of the infantry soldier in the 1914-18 war; images of men running a lighted match along the seams of their shirts were commonplace. I had never seen one but there were plenty of pictures so we knew what to look for. We were filthy, stinking and had fleas but I remain doubtful about lice, nevertheless the Army was going to delouse us anyway.

The method was foolproof. In the middle of the village square there was a set of chemical showers and to the side was a bonfire. We striped naked and threw all our clothes on the fire even though remember, we were now wearing our brand new uniforms only a few hours old; our Quartermaster was nowhere in sight of course. We raced through the showers and picked up second hand uniforms on the far side. The whole village, including a row of signorinas, stood and laughed at us. Some of the lads were very embarrassed and ran like hares across the square; I didn't though, I took my time and they gave me a cheer. After what we had been through how could a silly thing like this upset anyone?

We were no longer a Battalion, we were less than one hundred men; the three infantry Companies couldn't make a full Platoon. Woody, Palmer, Yank and I all stayed together through this unsettled period. We had all lost close friends. I remember with affection, Sergeant Wood (no relation of my mate Woody), we used to give him a hard time and call him an old bastard, but years later as I stood in front of his war grave, I found out that he was only twenty six. The cemetery was full of other colleagues, all under twenty years of age: it was a sad place.

Arthur Wood was still my closest friend but Palmer had the edge over us all; he had a talent which we lacked: he could drive, and he never let us forget it.
"Lets go to Naples tonight. We can pinch a car to get back in because I can drive."

We never used his services; the Army laid on transport called Liberty Buses, so there was no need. 'Banger' Jackson was another character who survived the Anzio rout. He was our company cook and one day he came to us with a proposition. If we could get chickens or ducks he would see that our large share was kept separate; Yank and I took on the task. The war had moved north and the countryside around Naples was getting back to normal but now that the Germans had gone the Italian farmers were free to complain about us.

Chicken stealing needed a certain panache and Yank didn't have any. We found that out on our first attempt; using his .45 he blew the chicken to bits and sent the signorinas screaming in all directions: the farmer was round to the CO, rapidamente. I found a method on my own and it was very successful. I would creep up to the hen house late at night, get inside and take the birds off the perch, put them in a sack and they never made a sound but it had to be very dark. One night though my plan did go wrong. As I approached the farm I heard a roaring sound like an 88mm shell. I knew there were none in the area but I threw myself down automatically. The roaring stopped and a huge dog came out of the darkness, stopped dead in mid-air two feet above me and then shot back into the night with a gasp and a squeal. A loose chain encircled the building and the dog was chained to a free running ring. It was the sound of the ring screaming along the chain that had caused me to throw myself flat. I was lucky that I was outside the limit of the chain when the dog jumped. He had put the chain under tension and shot back like a yo-yo.

In addition to my role as top chicken taker I tried my hand at milking. Some of the guys thought that it was strange, drinking milk straight from the cow while it was still warm but I thought it was delicious. All this larking about couldn't last though and rumours began to circulate. We might be going on leave; this was unbelievable unless we were going to Blighty for the invasion of Europe because good quality cannon fodder like us couldn't be wasted. The upshot of all the talk was that we were going to have our leave in Egypt and down to Taranto for embarkation we went.

Two months later there was an invasion of Europe and the Second Front was born: no more headlines for us, they were not going to use us on that one. Meanwhile we were in Taranto and the usual signs had been put up barring Black Cats from going into town. Two MPs caught four of us in a red light district, the Sergeant told his Corporal to book us then he walked off leaving his mate to cope. When the Corporal started to write us up, Woody dashed off the same way as the Sergeant. Within two minutes he was back,
"He's just gone into a brothel."
"Right," and following Woody's lead we went down to the house.
When the Sergeant appeared he was still doing up his flies and he had a shock to see us. He started to take it out on the Corporal so as we stood there we chanted,
"We won't tell if you don't," and that was the end of that.
Like I've said before, there's not much you can do with types like us. Not much fun in Taranto then, so let's see what Egypt had to offer; onto a troopship and we set sail for Port Said.

It was daylight when we sailed into the Port and from the top deck of the troop ship we had a good view of the city. The harbour was at least one mile across and full of ships anchored to mooring buoys. Causeways were floated out to the ships which were being unloaded. I was interested in Egyptian and Roman history at school and wish I had taken more advantage of the situation that presented itself. It would be many years before I could afford this kind of travel but I was the same as all the other guys and wanted to get to the low-life in the city with all possible speed.

Our leave was to start in Cairo but when we were told, "Not today," the prospect of more days on board did not go down well with the lads. Anchored in the harbour with the city so close, alternatives were discussed and plans made. Swim ashore as soon as it gets dark, that sounded reasonable to me but we are sixty feet above the water so it needed checking out. None of my mates were keen and I finished up with a bunch of Fusiliers. We checked out the ship together and the best bet was a loading bay on the lee side of the ship. The hatch was ten feet wide and fifteen feet above the water. One of our people knew the guy on guard so we got all the facts. Loading and unloading went on all day, the hatch was not closed at night but it was guarded by one of our own, not MPs, so far so good. Another alternative was to climb down the fore or aft anchor chains. We had a look and decided it would be easy to climb up if we had to. We parted company after we had made plans to meet up after dinner. Tropical Kit had been issued and the rules were no shorts after sunset and sleeves rolled down; this lightweight gear would be ideal in the water.

There were many men standing around the hatch and the guard wasn't happy but we convinced him that all he had to do was to let down the scramble net when we got back. It was very dark and we waited for the first one to jump. It wasn't me and several others had already chickened out at this stage. When I heard the splash, in I went with the rest of them. The sea wall was about 200 yards away and with our boots tied around our necks, we struck out. Twenty-five minutes later we are sitting on the wall steaming. There were ten of us and as no more came we set out for the town at a steady jog. Less than two miles and we were in the centre.

The first problem was money and getting the Arabs to accept wet Italian notes. They did but the deal had to be well in their favour; so drinks were going to be expensive. We attracted a lot of attention so we moved around before the MPs got interested. As for belly dancers and the like, we had neither the time nor the money. As a night out it was a flop but we would make it sound good when we got back. After a few hours of nothing in particular, we decided to go back to the ship; we would have to get our kicks out of lying to the others about what a marvellous time we had had.

After making sure no one was missing, we walked back to the sea wall. Our enthusiasm had waned and even the ship looked further away than when we left. Port Said was not blacked out like London or Coventry; the Egyptians were not subjected to nightly bombing like our people back home and the reflection on the water enabled us to see our way. There was no movement on the well lit deck and after one more look we slipped quietly into the water. Swimming round under the hatchway attracted no attention, so we called out. If we made too much noise there would be trouble and quiet shouting was difficult, time was getting on and it would soon be light. One of the guys said,
"Let's try the anchor chain," so three of us left the others and swam away.

The distance to the buoy plus half the length of the ship and we were beginning to tire. When we scrambled onto the platform to get our breath, we had a shock. Looking down from the deck in daylight, the chain looked an easy challenge but now on a pitching platform with a huge steel ring flopping about, things were very different. The chain went up at forty-five degrees, disappeared into the night and then appeared again under the lights on the deck. There was a sag in the middle and every time the ship rolled the chain twanged like a fiddle string; anyone holding on would be flung a hundred feet into the air. Not only that, the links opened and closed like nut crackers, so even if you survived the trapeze act you would lose fingers and toes on the climb: it was not an option.

It was getting noisy amidships and something was happening, so into the water we went, to join them. The lads were splashing around and no one was paying any attention. There was nothing on the side of the ship to hold on to and there was no chance to take a breather; some of the guys needed help. We all came to the same conclusion, it was no good trying the quiet approach, we'd have to make a lot of noise and to hell with it. A unified shout caused some faces to appear at the hatch but our pleas for a net or rope ladder were ignored. What are they playing at? Officers looked down then disappeared; we trod water and waited. After what seemed like hours a decision was made and we felt the full benefit of it. All the garbage in the ship poured out, not only rotten fruit but also excreta from the heads. We learned later that the Captain himself had given the order for the discharge.

Imagine what the environmentalists would say today; using the toilet whilst the train was standing in the station had nothing on this but there was a war on and we were winning, so nobody dared tell a Navy Captain what he could or couldn't do. Finally the net came down and we climbed up, stinking and tired. The whole ship's company hung over the rails to watch our humiliation. We stood in line whilst the MPs took our names and told about us the dire consequences.

Who knew what would happen, it was still very early in the morning.

I was the only one in our Company to try the midnight swim so there was no sympathy from the others about the possible charges against me but when the orders came to get ready to disembark, I made out that it was because of our escapade. The powers above got a move on to avoid any other incidents but they said I wouldn't be going with the others anyway because I could be charged with desertion. In the event there was no follow up by the MPs so I joined the paymaster's queue to get my back pay, which was considerable. I explained to the others they would be paid in piastres, a currency I was already familiar with having been ashore. However, the laughter ceased when an officer came to tell us that our leave in Cairo would only be three days. This was a blow but infantrymen have no choice. As we marched in single file away from the quay, I looked back at the steel sides of the ship and I realised how lucky I had been early that morning trying to get back on board.

Chapter 10

Summer Holidays

With more than two hundred miles to go, we settled down to a five hour journey with an escort of armed Military Police motorcyclists leading the way. Who could imagine that I would do the same journey fifty six years later, on a tourist bus with an armed escort? Nothing seems to change in the Arab world except that the motorcycles and the guns get bigger, naturally.

Into the metropolitan city of Cairo we came. If you compared it with Blackpool we went to the St. Annes' equivalent part called Heliopolis. We marched down the centre of a road with large Victorian type houses on both sides. A Billeting Officer met us and referring to his list, he peeled us off in sixes and sevens, directing us to our places. Ours was not to reason why, ours was but to wonder why - how the hell these people got such jobs. With a quick lecture on the do's and don'ts, he reminded us he would be back in three days and then handed us over to a Blackpool type landlady.

The landlady spoke no English but she repeated one of the don'ts the Billeting Officer had already dealt with, using her own anatomy as an aide to the sign language. She made it quite clear that no women were to enter the house. It was suggested that we proposition her, but nobody had the nerve. The woman problem was solved by our next visitor, a private soldier. Woody and I had moved into a room by the front door so that when the squaddie came in, we were the first he saw. He looked us over cautiously and decided we were ok. He asked us to go with him to see his set up. At the bottom of the road there were several large detached houses and we entered one of the gardens behind them. Our new friend was a batman to a Brigadier who was on the permanent staff at Cairo HQ: that explained the posh house.

"Don't worry," he said, "the Brig. never comes into the garden."

In a corner behind some shrubs there was a large shed; it was fitted out like a boudoir and it housed two quality dolly birds. This guy had his own private brothel.
"Is the Brigadier in on it?" I asked.
"No, only one of the servants in the house, he's a relation of the girls."
What initiative, this guy is going to rule the world I thought.
"So what do you need us for?" I said suspiciously.
"You guys change every three days and it looks bad if I go round to every house. I need someone to put the others in the picture."

Pimping for three days did not appeal to either of us so we told him that we would let as many know as possible and then we availed ourselves of the girls' services as a goodwill gesture. He thanked us and said that the girls were on the house.
We made our way back to the billet in high spirits, not a bad start for a holiday.

I can't believe how young I was

We did have a little bit of historical input. Nobody goes to Cairo without seeing the Pyramids but Cheops, Chephren and Menkaura were names that meant nothing to me. Pyramids are what you see, huge stone tombs. We spent the day climbing up the one with the top bit missing, standing on the flat shouting at each other. The camel rides and baksheesh went without saying. How different years later when, on business for the Egyptian Government, I met an American Egyptologist who was studying Cheops. He took me in the King's Chamber and I helped to set up an X-ray machine to scc if there were any more hidden passages. I never found out the result as I had to leave for Aswan before he finished.

In 1944 my mind was on other things. The night life in Cairo was all a young soldier could wish for. The first clubs we went into set the scene. Escort girls met you at the door and you had to buy them a drink before they would sit down. The drink was coloured water at an exorbitant price and the entertainment was on a stage in the corner behind a steel mesh. The reason for the mesh was obvious. When a fight broke out the band kept playing, oblivious to the flying bottles. Fights were usually between Canadians, Americans, Australians and British even though we were all on the same side. Only the Arab businessmen were winning as they were fully compensated for all the damage, but it was all good fun. The big posh shops had a different agenda to the markets and I am reminded of an incident when Woody was trying to knock down the price on something for his girlfriend at home in Stoke. The salesman was standing his ground,

"We are not a bushaar sir, I suggest you try the Souk."

Whilst this was going on, a smartly dressed Egyptian wearing a Fez, like Tommy Cooper [Tommy got the Fez idea while entertaining the troops in the desert] stopped to explain why my friend was having so much trouble. His English was perfect and I have to say he did impress me. When Woody finally joined us we were well into politics and difficulties caused by the crisis. He said his own family had been reduced to replenishing their fortunes in a way that was unheard of before the war.

"In what way?" I asked.

"My own beautiful sister has to be a host at parties for government officials." He looked sad. "It is not right for people of our rank to expose their woman in this way."

I sympathized with all my heart but my mind was still on the beautiful sister, so we talked on, had a coffee and got even more friendly. I worked the conversation round to the possibility of meeting his family. I really thought I was in control. We didn't want to inconvenience all of them of course just his sister would be nice. He didn't think that would be possible as she only met high ranking officers so it would be embarrassing for her.

"Couldn't she make an exception in our case. We only have two more days in Cairo." I said in my best 'touch the forelock style'.

"Ok, I'll see what I can do. Let's get a taxi."

Woody watched me carefully but did not say anything; I thought that I was still in control. I should have realised all was not well by the little things, but at seventeen I knew it all.

Normally a taxi driver only wants to know the address and off you go but our posh friend was having a long conversation in Arabic with the driver and even the sly looks he kept throwing in our direction didn't register in my over active mind. The three of us got into the battered cab and we went a long, long way. Even when Woody made a remark about passing the same mosque twice, I told him to shut up.

"Cairo is a big place and don't try to spoil everything."

Finally we stopped in a wide street with official looking buildings on one side. The taxi driver looked to me for the fare. It was a lot of money so I started to argue; our Egyptian friend took over and the price was reduced. The driver went away unhappy and the look on his face made me feel that I had won but I had still paid a lot of money for what turned out to be a very short journey. We walked a few yards and our escort stopped; he still looked sad.

"I don't think I can do this," he said, "my sister can be very difficult."

"Perhaps you could offer her this ten pounds for her dowry," I said, holding out the note.

He said nothing but he took the note from my hand. Up until now, Woody had let me run with the ball but

now he made a remark,
"Hold on, how do we know we can trust this guy?"
The whole scene changed and hostilities began immediately.
"Trust me! How dare you. You have insulted my honour. I want nothing more to do with you."

Like I said before, it's the little things. He still had my £10 in his hand; shouldn't he have thrown it in Woody's face before he walked away? I still hadn't got the big picture. I rounded on my colleague,
"Now look what you've done, you've fucked it all up."
I ran after the Egyptian shouting apologies. He turned to face me and in the next few minutes I did my very best.
"My friend didn't mean to be offensive, he's had some bad experiences with some of your Countrymen and he is very sorry."
He held up the ten pound note in front of my face and he said, "My father is a Bey and you expect me to go to my sister with this."
"A Bey?" I thought, what the hell is that, but I said, "A Bey. I should have known. I am very sorry."

That seemed to simplify matters; perhaps it was my ten pounds rather than Arthur's remark which had upset him. I produced two more £10 notes. The snob in me was running away with my reason. Thirty pounds was seven months pay in Infantry terms. He took the notes from my hand and looked down the road at Woody.
"What about him?" he said.
"I'll go and talk to him, it will be ok."
When I got to my reluctant colleague he said,
"You've given him more money, haven't you?"
"Yes, but don't worry, I've squared everything. Did you know his father is a Bey?"
"A Bey, what the hell is that?"
"I don't know but it must be something high up. His sister may be a princess or something."

We walked back to our host. I know now that the only reason he waited was because Woody may have been good for another thirty quid, but there was no chance of that. Now the pot was empty, he carried on with his original plan.

"Getting my sister to meet two British Army privates is going to be difficult. Give me a few minutes to talk to her." He raised his eyes to the top of the building. I imagined a luxury flat full of eastern promise.

"Wait five minutes and I'll call you."

He went up the few steps, opened the large door and disappeared. We fidgeted about for the next five minutes, then Woody went up to the door and pushed it open. I was surprised it was not locked. He disappeared for a minute then his head came round the door and he shouted,

"Princess my arse."

I ran up to him, thinking instead of a glamour girl I was going to meet some dirty scrubber but no, it was worse. I was going to meet nobody. I stood there in amazement and looked around, it was nothing but rubble. The backs of several buildings had been bulldozed. The fronts may have had some historic value so they had been left.

"He has got away with our money." I gasped.

"Your money," corrected Woody. We went into the street and walked a little way looking at the buildings.

"How could we have fallen for this"? I murmured.

If you looked at the top windows it was obvious that there was no roof on.

"You fell for it," corrected Woody once more. He was not gong to let me off easily. Our eyes were everywhere hoping to spot the con-man. He could have gone in any one of twenty different ways from the building so we had little hope. Perhaps it was just as well, because I had murder in my heart.

We went back to the shop in the main road where we had met the con-man. It was a very short journey; the taxi man had done very well out of me. There were battered taxi cabs all over Cairo and it was always a battle when it was time to pay but our guy won that one.

It was our second day in the capital and I can't remember anything particular after our brush with the swindler, until it was time to go and catch the Liberty truck. The pick up system worked very well, there were several collection points around the city to take us back free of charge. A small number of men were waiting when we arrived and after a short time Palmer and a mate joined us.

"Hey Woody, I've been telling my mate here, there's no need to wait for a lift." We knew what was coming next. "Let's pinch a car and go back to camp in style, I can drive."
Why not we thought and we followed him up the road. We were looking half-heartedly at prospective automobiles when Palmer's mate said,
"Why bother, let's grab one of those," he was pointing at a Garry that had just passed us.
Garries were quite common in Arab towns; a four seater carriage drawn by a half starved horse.
"How do you say 'giddy up' in Arabic," I said, trying to be smart.
"No problem, I was on a milk round for three years before I joined up."
We took a fresh look at our comrade in arms. Palmer's deal was completely forgotten.
"Look, there's a row of them waiting for fares," said the milkman.

There was a wide bridge over the river Nile with two lion statues at the entrance. Next to the statues five carriages stood by the curb with chocks under the wheels, the drivers were sitting in a group talking.

"Pay attention," said the milkman, "walk along the curb to the lead carriage."

We were now in single file, infantry style.

"When I get level, I'll grab the whip out of the holster and get onboard, one of you kick out the chock and all get on quickly."

Before we had time to think about it, he had made his move. I had to kick hard at the chock because the horse was already pulling. While still on the running board looking back, I could see the drivers running into the road and start to give chase.

"Get a move on, they're on to us," I shouted as I climbed onto the back seat.

There were two more lions at the far end of the bridge, we cleared those and the horse got into its stride; things were under control.

"Where to, where to," our milkman cried. He wanted some directions on where to deliver us.

"Keep going, we'll sort something out." We knew that there would be trouble if we took it all the way and we were attracting too much attention. So we tied the horse to a lamppost and hitched a ride on one of the many Liberty trucks back to Heliopolis.

Our third day in Cairo passed without incident, unless I mention the tattoo caper. Most men in the Army and Navy had tattoos; they cost as little as a shilling in some towns. Mine was a small bird with a scroll in its beak with the name Dorothy on it but because it was in two colours, it had cost 2/3d [around 11 pence]. The artist was a guy in Colchester who had a shop with modern equipment. In Cairo the tattooist just sat in the dirt. It was near to the market but he didn't qualify for a stall. He had gathered a small crowd and a squaddie sat beside him with his arm held out. The squaddie was pulling faces and the others were taking the mickey out of his torment. "Bloody pansies," I said. They turned round and saw my shoulder tab.

"The pussycats are here now, they are going to show

us how tough they are."

I smarted at that remark and spoke to my mate, "Go on Woody, you haven't got one, show them how it's done."

He hesitated only a second then nodded to the Arab. It's difficult to explain peer pressure but it's easier to go along than to stand your ground and I was pointing at my tattoo. The Arab handed Woody an indelible pencil; he licked the end of it and made a blue line on his arm. You were expected to draw your own design. The guy in Colchester had a whole wall full of transfers, you just picked one out, stuck it on your arm and the tattooist made a copy over it. Woody drew a scroll and put the word Mother in it.

"Isn't that nice," the others said sarcastically.

There was a gasp of relief when the Arab finished with his client and the squaddie stood up holding his bleeding limb. Woody sat down and held out his arm; five seconds later he was on his feet,

"Christ Almighty, no way," he shouted.

The tattooist had only gone ¼ inch along the scroll. The onlookers had a field day, shouting, "Pussy, pussy." The Arab was laughing, he was being paid whether he finished or not. This looked bad for The Black Cat Division.

"Gimme the fucking pencil," I cried. This was a matter of honour. I had to lick the pencil several times but I was quite proud of my artistry. Three pyramids, a palm tree and the sun coming up.

I pointed to the sun and said to the Arab, "I want that in bright red understand?"

We agreed on a price and I sat down. In Colchester, the man had used electric equipment, with a needle that entered the skin a thousand times a minute at a controlled depth. There was an unpleasant burning feeling but it was not too painful, if you had a large design it was done in stages over several weeks. For the first time I had a good look at the tackle the Arab was using. The needle was held in a split bamboo cane, bound with twine so it could not move, he had a little hammer and the ink was contained in four dirty saucers - blue, yellow, red and green. The whole lot was laid out on a filthy piece of rag on the sand. A finer kit for spreading hepatitis all over Egypt could not be found anywhere but there was no turning back now.

My arm lay across his knee; he lined up the needle on the base of the pyramid and gave it a tap, before I could gasp he tapped it another five times and moved about ¼ inch. He was very skilled and there was no chance of him nailing my arm to his leg. He tapped and tapped, my arm was covered with blood which he wiped away with a dirty piece of cloth. I quickly changed this for my own clean handkerchief, which would shorten the odds of infection by fifty percent. After he had finished the outline of the Pyramid, he started to fill in the block work. I hadn't bothered with this detail but he was going to get it right. Christ, I had a palm tree and a blazing Sun to go yet; this macho thing is going too far. Then it was all over. When my masterpiece healed it should be there forever, for all to see. Tattooing was allowed in the Services but if you reported sick it could be regarded as a self-inflicted wound and that could mean trouble if you were about to go into action. There was though an unusual post-script to all this tattooing business.

In the 1970s, I had some work from an Egyptian Arms company and I was staying at the Mena House, near Cairo. The Mena House was a wooden hotel for officers during the war but when I was there, it was a four star modern complex. The manger asked me to share my room with another Englishman, as it would help him over a booking cock-up. I wasn't very keen but he introduced me anyway. The man was the manager of the famous Blackpool Trams and he was writing a book about transport. His wife didn't travel with him but every year she booked him into a Country with interesting trams. So far, she'd sent him to Mexico, China, Peru and now he was in Egypt to film some old Polish trams. His other claim to fame was that he was a friend of Alistair Cook, the famous 'Letter from America' radio correspondent. I couldn't resist all this; of course he could share my room. When you are an ordinary chap like me with no connection with celebrities, you grasp every opportunity that comes along however remote and Alistair Cooke was a favourite of mine. It's no worse than the woman who knew a man who knew a woman who had a friend who had danced with the Prince of Wales.

The next day I shared a taxi with him and we headed into the City with cameras. We wandered around the old part of the town and got separated for a while. I had trams on the mind when I stood on an old tramline with a tram coming slowly towards me, could it be Polish? It was packed inside and out with people and those clinging on the outside made it lean outwards. When two passed each other they would form a giant V; right tram or not, this was a good picture. I raised the camera but before I could click, the pole broke and the tram shuddered to a halt. There must have been a hundred people in and on that tram; they rushed towards me and surrounded me. I was aware of the tension between Israel and Egypt because of the recent war and I was very concerned when they shouted, "Israeli, Israeli."

It was stupid of me to use the camera like that; an uncontrolled Arab mob is a frightening thing and I shouted at the top of my voice,
"Police, Police."
Two armed soldiers pushed their way though the crowd. They spoke no English and punched me about repeating, "Israeli."
"Not Israeli, friend of Egypt," and I showed them the Pyramids on my arm.
This confused these two simple soldiers and I followed

up my luck by pointing at their shoulder tabs and shouting,
"I want Officer, Officer," and finally they got the picture.

The crowd were going mad and pushing each other out of the way to try and get a look at my arm until thankfully the soldiers took me off to a patrol post. I didn't care what they did as long as I got away from that mob.

They locked me in the guardroom; I sat at a table and waited and waited. The officer came into the room with an attitude,
"You're an Israeli propaganda spy." The fact that he spoke good English didn't seem to help.
"How can I be Israeli with this thing on my arm," I said, showing him my tattoo.
It had worked before but not this time.
"That doesn't mean anything. Israeli's are very devious."
"Look, I work for Egypt. My agent is an ex-Army General in your Army."
That gave him food for thought but I had to be careful.

The Israelis had given the Egyptians a thrashing which was probably why my agent was an ex. I explained about my missing tram friend and he left the room to give orders to someone. When he returned, some time later, it was obvious that my colleague had not been found.
"Why don't you check with my hotel? There are papers there to prove what I'm saying."
He left the room again and I waited and waited and waited. When he returned he had my camera in his hand, which he handed to me. With a grim look on his face he said,
"Come with me."
I was worried but there was no problem. We went outside and walked a few streets, he stopped and

pointed to a building,
"You like that?"
"Yes."
"Take pictures then."
We moved on and stopped in front of a Mosque
"You like that?"
"Yes."
"Take pictures then."
This happened so many times that I didn't bother to
wind the film on and just pretended to click. When he
was satisfied he said,
"There are so many beautiful things in Egypt there is
no need to film bad things," then he walked away.

I thought that my tattoos were for life but my wife had
other ideas, not just because one of them said Dorothy
and her name was Jessica but because only yobs had
tattoos. The fact that the Duke of Norfolk and Lord
Litchfield had them made no difference.
"Yobs," she said.
"What can I do about it, they're permanent."
They stayed with me until 1985 but my wife never
gave up. She saw an article in a medical journal,
"Tattoos removed by laser." I was booked into the
Nuffield Hospital immediately at £85 per visit. It's a
painful procedure, the laser burns off the skin. After
three visits, the Pyramids were gone but the bird was
proving more difficult. I didn't turn up for my forth
appointment so some of the bird remains but there's
no Dorothy now. My wife let it go at that. I wasn't a
kid anymore and couldn't take that kind of discomfort;
it wasn't the same as in 1944.

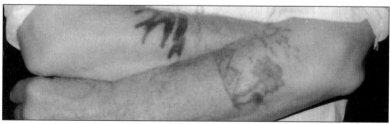

The tattoos which years later saved my life

Chapter 11

Yes, We Have No Bananas

Back in 1944, the only future that concerned us was the next few weeks. The Cairo leave was over and the Billeting Officer, still waving his bits of paper about, marched us off to the waiting transport. Our destination was Ismailia, by the Suez Canal. This was good news as we had expected to go straight to Italy and be back in action within a few days.

It was a large camp and well organized; the tents were set up with military precision and we were very close to the town. There were the remains of several Infantry Regiments in the camp but wherever possible we kept to our own kind. On our first visit to the town, we had trouble. There were 'Out of Bounds' signs everywhere. This attitude, 'You can die for us, but you can't walk up our street', always put us in a bad mood, so we took no notice. The fight started in a large coffee house; every Arab in the place was having a go at the four of us, it was quite nasty. When the knives came out I think my action saved the day. I jumped on the counter and put my arms around a large elaborate vase and started to shake it. The proprietor was screaming at me in Arabic, I think he was telling me to be careful with his most prized possession. There was a lull in the fighting as the proprietor calmed them down. I pointed at the door and said,
"We go...."
"Ya, ya," and he started pushing customers away from the door.
We left the building but there was a crowd waiting for us in the street and they started throwing stones at us. When an Arab mob starts stoning its very nasty, there was always so much ammunition about because of all the rubble. We ran for our lives, in and out of the narrow alleyways. I ran up a ruined building onto

the roof and after crossing several houses, disturbing the woman doing their chores, I jumped down into the street straight into the arms of two Military Policemen.

After the war I worked at the Triumph Motor Cycle Company and I met a guy who was in the Military Police in Ismailia and he told me they had an observation post in one of the towers. They had watched us squaddies come into the Arab quarter all the time.

"We would give you enough time to start some bother and then go and arrest you."
These two that had me were certainly laughing. Being charged by the MPs meant going in front of the CO, so the next morning I had my excuse ready.
"Quick march, right turn, stand still," bawled the Sergeant Major.
"What have you to say for yourself, Darlington?"
"It was the bananas, sir."
"Bananas?"
"Yes, sir. I bought some Bananas and the trader ran off with my change. I gave chase and didn't realise he had gone into the Arab quarter."
"Did you catch him?"
"No, sir. There was a crowd causing trouble so I had to give up the chase."
"I see."
"I even lost my bananas, sir."
"All right, that's enough. Extra guard duty. Wheel him out Sergeant Major."
"About turn, quick march, left turn..."

Enjoying a banana in Cairo, a luxury not possible in Britain in 1944

Extra duty meant patrolling the camp at night. There was no perimeter fence, so pilfering by boys from the town was commonplace. Stealing from the British was considered an honourable profession by the Arabs. One night the padre had things stolen from under his camp bed while he was asleep. He was very upset, they could have cut his throat at the same time; that was the risk which you took when you had a camp bed and a tent all to yourself. Other ranks slept on the sand, several to a tent; if an Arab entered, the risk was all his.

The theft of the padre's possessions was a serious breach of security and the desert Arabs were thought to be the culprits, so special trackers were sent for. The Arab trackers were very colourful, their uniforms and camels were highly decorative like Moroccan Scouts and they looked very efficient as they went off across the desert. Some time later they returned with a scruffy gang of Arabs running behind them, all roped together. How many does it take to rob a Padre, we wondered? They recovered none of the goods, they would keep that for themselves and it's doubtful if they had the right people in any case. All of this was obvious to the ranks but the officers had difficultly in catching on to the nitty gritty of Arab low life!

The next bit of excitement in this boring camp was because Woody had an idea. He had found out about a Signals course for volunteers. The course took place at a camp near by called Beni Yousef. Woody had done it back home,
"Piece of cake," he said.
"I can't cope with that," I offered.
"Yes you can, stick with me."
The Signals Officer gave us a talk about procedure and handed out sheets of paper with Morse Code and other things we were supposed to learn.
"I don't expect you to become signallers, just learn the basics and Morse up to five words a minute," the Officer encouraged.
"I can't cope with this Woody, there's bound to be a test."
"If there is sit by me and copy mine." He sounded so confident.

Reluctantly I signed up for the course, although there was another good reason for doing so. A jeep was made available so that we could space ourselves out in the desert for radio practice. Out of sight of any authority, racing round exploring the mysteries of the gearbox was much more fun than radios. Palmer was going to lose his edge and at least it saved me from all the sand bashing and other bullshit that went on in this boring place.

Signalling at Company level was done with an 18 Set. It was a large radio carried on the back with a handset for sending messages. It could also pick up dance music and the like, so on the pretence of needing it for practice we borrowed one for each tent. There were six tents set up well away from the main camp. On the weekend, while the others were marching up and down and went on Church Parade, we lay on our backs and listened to the radio.

Someone had to spoil it though, didn't they? The lady was about to hit a high note when someone who didn't like opera switched over to 'send' and shouted,
"Get off the air you fat old cow."
Whether the lady was fat or not we shall never know but what we did find out was the message came out loud and clear in a Senior Officers' Mess in the posh part of town. Apparently Brigadiers and Colonels who hadn't seen action since 1914 were incensed, after all there were ladies present.
"Find that man and have him thrashed," was the cry.

When it was explained that flogging wasn't allowed any more the Military Police took on the case with a more practical approach, like checking out everyone who had access to an 18 Set over the weekend. Eventually they landed on our doorstep or tent flap, as the case maybe. There were six tents and every tent had a set, about twenty five men were involved, we stood in line and let Woody do the talking.
"We send and receive to the other tents, to practice the procedure sir."
"What do you talk about?"
"We read from the standard text sir."
"No obscenities?"
"Not unless it's in the text sir."

"You know what I mean, don't muck about."

"Yes sir." Woody was doing well and we kept a straight face.

"What about frequency, do you change it about?"

"No sir, we only use the ones we're trained for."

The officer addressed the whole company.

"Do any of you know anything about this business at 13.50 hours on Sunday?"

"No sir," was the chorus.

It could have been anyone in a forty mile radius of Ismailia.

That was the end of the investigation; it was also the end of the Signals course. I suppose we looked guiltier than anyone else but it definitely had nothing to do with us. We would have thrashed the person responsible if we knew who it was. I was apprehensive about the course at first but it was a cushy number and now it was back to all the bullshit.

From the little information that came to us, it seemed the war in Italy was not going too well. Cassino was holding on against massive attacks and the German Paratroopers were driving back the New Zealand and Indian troops. Anzio wasn't doing much better; the German 14th Army was still keeping up the pressure, so we were sure they would be sending us into action soon. The camp with all its bullshit and boring discipline was still a better option than Italy. Any scheme that would keep us there longer was good, so we listened carefully to the officer.

The desert victory had been won mainly with tanks and heavy artillery. The Italian country with its mountains, rivers and dense population was not suitable for the same tactics: infantry was the thing but the infantry absorbed men like a sponge, as we all knew to our cost. Hundreds of artillerymen were being transferred into infantry Regiments and the NCOs were allowed to keep their stripes only if they went on an infantry course. The officer went on to explain

108

how we would be part of the grand plan and play the enemy. Three truck loads of pseudo Germans headed for the depot to be kited out. There was no ordnance, the German equipment was in separate piles and we rummaged about until we found something that fitted. There were hundreds of Jackboots and helmets but finding a jacket with some rank on the epaulettes was difficult.

Officers urged us to get a move on and shouted,
"You'll find no Generals gear among that lot."
We stood in rows and officers came round to see what we proposed to wear. Someone said,
"There's no tropical kit, we'll be too hot."
"The NCOs won't be seeing anyone in tropical kit where they're going, stupid man."
"But will the NCOs we're chasing be wearing tropical kit sir?"
"What anyone else is wearing is of no concern of yours, now shut up."
He pointed to a group of officers,
"Those men will be acting as marshals. Now put your kit on and let them see what you look like."
Five men to a marshal, that was the drill. A Major came to talk to us like we were idiots. Woody, Palmer, me and two lads from the old Company stood by his Jeep, five men in anticipation.
"The NCOs will be firing blanks. You will be using live ammo, that is why you are keeping your own rifles, to minimise accidents. Any questions?"
We looked at each other and thought, "What a pratt," then tried to outdo each with question time.
"You are expecting accidents then, sir?"
"I did not say that; there will be no accidents." My turn next,
"There is always a percentage of causalities allowed in a field exercise, sir."
"There will be no causalities, is that perfectly clear."
"So you want us to bang our guns and fire in the air, sir."

"No I want you be realistic and safe."

"We can't put the German bayonet on the rifle to do a realistic charge, sir?"

"There will be no close engagement with the enemy, do you understand?"

We all looked at Palmer; come on son we want a gem from you.

"In the event of an accident sir, how would you know who was responsible?"

"For God's sake, what's the matter with you people, there will be no accidents. If there is you will all be charged together, now shut up and get in the Jeep."

He drove for an hour until we came to a green area by a long irrigation canal with smaller ditches being fed by the usual donkey walking round a rag and chain pump.

"Is that the Suez Canal sir?"

"No it's not; don't start all that again just pay attention."

I looked at this Major, he was another one; him and his mates running around the desert with squaddies in a Jeep; the most danger they faced was a burst tyre. It never ceased to amaze me, the jobs that were available if you were in the know.

"The enemy will come from that direction, you will harass them for half an hour then retreat." He pointed from West to East.

"Keep this up for the rest of the day, I shall be checking up on you."

"What about grub sir?" Palmer was trying to have the last word.

"You will assume that it's battlefield conditions and act accordingly."

With that he climbed into the Jeep and as he moved off his last remark was,

"No accidents."

A few Arabs stood around and watched us suspiciously. I suggested we scout around to find out where they

110

were coming from. About half a mile away in the same direction as the enemy, we could see an oasis and a village. We agreed to take a look and remembering my own experience with date jam I issued a warning,
"Only eat fruit with a thick skin and don't touch the desert women."
"Why?"
"Well it's obvious about the fruit and the women may be Berbers and their men can be touchy, that's what I've read any way."
When we got into the village we goose-stepped around shouting, "The British are finished." The villagers took no notice; it didn't matter to them who was in charge. Palmer was the first to spot the sand cloud,
"Look, we're in business."
"Nobody said they would be mechanized."
"They're not, it's two Jeeps, probably got marshals bringing up the rear."
Woody made the best suggestion,
"Let's make sure they're using blanks before we do anything silly."
We had to show ourselves before they got too close in. As soon as we heard the bangs, we hit the sand and watched the palm tree leaves.
"It's ok, they are blanks all right."
"Right, now let's have some fun."

We hid ourselves in the muddy ditches and waited. Some of the Arab kids were watching us so we waved them away but they took no notice. A couple of shots in the palm trees above their heads soon scattered them and some elders rushed over and took them out of the area. The firing had made the NCOs stop and take better cover. I don't know what our enemy had been told to expect but they seemed to be taking a long time to make a move. We crawled in the ditches until we were all together in a bunch, something we would never do if there was a real enemy; one hand grenade would have seen us all off. The general opinion was that we didn't want to sit there all day.

"We've been told to harass them, so let's do it," suggested Palmer who was soaking wet. He had fallen into the water and had had trouble finding his glasses.

"Fell in the drink have you Pammy."

"Never mind about that, let's sort out these wankers and get out of here."

"I don't want to do time because one of you bastards was trigger happy."

Always the sensible approach from Woody. He was looking at me when he said it and I suppose he was thinking about the Arab in North Africa in '43.

It was the officer's fault for not making it clear who was in charge. We wouldn't have taken much notice of anyone but it would have been useful in a stalemate like this; I decided to have my say.

"Look, you can take a lot of liberties with a guy using blanks, so let's frighten them to death and make them run."

"There's a Jeep out there watching us."

"There are two Jeeps somewhere but they are marshals and they won't interfere."

There was unanimous agreement, without anyone actually saying, "let's go." We spread out along the channel and moved towards them. The NCOs had had the same idea and we met head-on. We took some pot shots in the confines of the channel and there was a mad scramble as they tried to get out of the ditch. They ran across the sand looking for new ditches to jump into and we jumped in as well, pumping bullets into the side of the banks.

Woody was shouting, "For God's sake be careful."

They made an attempt to set up a Bren gun but we ignored its blank fire and the crew started to run with the others. With bullets kicking up sand at their running feet we were firing very close, too close. The second jeep appeared from behind some trees and the marshal told us to stop.

The Captain seemed a decent sort, "Good show lads, now break off. We may catch up with you later."
When we went back to the village we got more respect from the inhabitants, the kids had been giving glowing reports about our victory over the British; it was mint tea all round.
We didn't think that we would see anymore of the enemy, so we wandered around the village to kill time; it was going to be a boring afternoon. We never did explain ourselves to the villagers and they must have been very confused. Palmer was going on about the heat and the uniforms.
"If only we could find some transport."
"We all know you can drive."
"It's worth a try, let's have a good search."
"You've more chance of finding King Farouk than a car in this place."

I looked at the donkey carts but we didn't have the milkman with us and the animals looked so starved. We walked about three miles along the canal until it finished up as a mud hole. In the far distance we could see the superstructure of large ships moving through the sand. To see these unnatural objects moving through the sand dunes was an amazing sight. We debated whether to take a closer look at the Suez Canal but it was too far and we were not dressed in suitable kit for a trek across soft sand, so it was back to the comfort of the green area. The NCOs had one more try but it was half-hearted and they headed off to the West.
Someone said, "Now what?"
"Just take your jacket off and lie in the shade, they'll pick us up soon."
With a good swig of water we did just that. It was me that spotted the jeep coming over the sand.
"It's that pratt Major coming back, get dressed."
"I bet he'll check our water bottles," said Woody.
Of course he will, water discipline was very strict in the desert and I'd drunk all mine.

"You're probably right Woody, I'd better play safe."
I jumped down to the bottom of the ditch and filled my bottle with the dirty water. The jeep pulled up and we stood round expecting to be taken back. This pompous Major was in no hurry, he stood up on the seat and said,
"It's hot!"
"Not for you it's not," we all thought but nobody said it aloud. He glanced round, not even looking at us, put out his arm and said,
"Give me a bottle."
I was the only one standing on the off side, the other four were over by the driver. The Major didn't look to see who was on the end of his arm, "Come on man," he said to the sky.
I hesitated, the lads were starring at me, they knew what was on my mind then the officer looked down for the first time,
"Have you gone to sleep, having a nap are you?"
I unclipped the bottle and handed it over. He unscrewed the cap and took a hefty swig.
He sputtered, spat and shouted, "What's the matter with this, it tastes like shit."
I looked up at the pompous bastard and I couldn't hold back my remark,
"Well it would sir; I just filled it up down there."
Still standing on the seat he turned his head and looked down at the green slime, his eyes stood out like pigeon eggs,
"You did what?"
He screamed out the words and sat down with a crash, jammed in the gears and raced across the desert.
"He's pissed off with you Golly."
"Sod him, the pompous pig."
"He's going to leave us here to die of thirst now."
"We'll confiscate one of those village houses and live here for ever," I suggested.
"Could we get away with that?"
"Course we could, we're the super race."

We were in good form and didn't give a dam about the Major's problem. We found out later that the Major was, naturally, very concerned. A jeep drove up and down making clouds of dust, it was only two hundred yards away before we realised that it wasn't the Major.

The Sergeant said, "I've been looking all over for you lot, what have you been up to?"

"Nothing, Sarg." We were unanimous with our negative reply.

"Well something's wrong, there's a big stink back at base."

All of us were deep in thought as we drove back with him in silence. I had already made up my mind that none of the others would suffer for my behaviour. We stopped in front of the administration tent and no less than the Regimental Sergeant Major was waiting for us,

"Get out you krauts and stand up."

They always said stand up, like we were lying down or something. The RSM went on, "Trying to poison one of HM Officers is a serious offence, we could shoot you for that."

"Christ," I thought, I hope this guy has been properly briefed and not under the impression that we're real Germans. I could imagine him thinking, *"Caught five krauts trying to poison an officer, sah." "Good, put them up against a wall RSM, PDQ."*

I stepped smartly forward and said, "Nothing to do with these chaps sir, it was my prank."

"Prank was it. Right you four, clear off. You come with me." I walked behind him into the large tent.

"Are you going to charge me now sir?"

"Oh no, the CO wants to sort this out himself. Be outside his office at 09.00 hours in the morning. Best kit, stand up, dismiss."

I stood to attention and yelled, "Yes sir."

They had just made a mistake; if they had charged

me straight away I would have told them exactly what happened but now I had all night to think about it. When I was a little kid, my father nicknamed me, "Alibi Al" and a good excuse did save me from a lot of thrashings; by morning I could have taken the oath.

"Quick march, right turn, stand still." The CO sat there staring.

"This is a lot more serious than stealing bananas, Darlington."

"I didn't steal bananas sir, it was the trader that sto..."

"Never mind about all that, what about this charge the Major is making?"

"That was a joke, sir."

"Some joke, the water was poisoned."

"I don't understand that sir, it wasn't my water bottle."

"Not your water bottle? Explain yourself man?"

"To conserve water we were only using the one canteen sir, mine had not been used. I got the bottle from the German pile at the depot and filled it up the same as the others. There must have been something wrong with the bottle sir."

"The officer said you filled it from the ditch."

"That was my little joke sir, but before I could explain the Major drove off."

"I see." The CO was seriously thinking about this, so I decided to press on,

"Was the officer right to demand my water sir? He was in a jeep with plenty of his own. We had been in the sun all day chasing those NCOs."

"All right, don't keep on."

I knew that I was home and dry when the CO summed up,

"The Major went straight to the Medical Officer, so we'll await the outcome. If anything happens you'll be hearing more about this, dismiss."

"About turn, quick march."

The RSM was behind me and whispered, "You lucky sod."

It reminded me of a tale my uncle Dick used to tell. Because of a gas attack in the 1914 - 1918 war, he suffered all his life with lung trouble. Uncle claimed a Colonel had demanded his gas mask from him because he didn't have one and he was more important than my uncle, which he was; but they don't get away with it all the time.

Chapter 12

Back to Front

The news from Italy was all bad; the German 14th Army was still giving Anzio a hard time and Cassino was holding on against heavy but unsuccessful attacks by New Zealand and Indian troops. We were convinced that they would be sending us back into action soon. To make matters worse we had no more back up money, all the loot had been sold and wages were a standard fifty piastres every two weeks, just enough to get drunk on: it was a sad time.

We could have made something out of that NCO business; the German gear would have sold well but it was a one off and there was no time to organize. Some know-all said we were off in a couple of days and just in case he was right we decided to have a last piss-up in town. Woody, two Fusiliers and I made our way to the city to say our last 'inshallay'. Palmer and Yank made their own way. Woody thought that they had a bit of money and didn't want to share it but I think Palmer was out to get a car.

We walked about aimlessly like soldiers do when they don't have a plan, drinking the cheapest wine we could find and slowly getting drunk. The others were drunker than I was, I was still careful about what I put down my throat, that bout of dysentery in Libya had taught me a lesson. It was late in the evening and we were in the old Arab quarter, we could see a market, it looked lively and we approached. A few dim oil lamps illuminated the crowded stalls. There were no other Servicemen about and we had the usual strange looks from the Arabs. The two Fusiliers were staggering badly and Woody wasn't much better, then one of them started making remarks about women in bad Arabic. The figure came out of the gloom, his white

galabeya gave him a menacing presence.
With his hands behind his back he said, "Bint, Bint."

We all knew the word for woman and I moved forward to hear what he had to say. I was two yards away from him when he brought his arm round fast; he held a great bull whip in his hand. Taken completely by surprise the first blow knocked me down on my knees. Still in that position, he laid into me until I fell on my face but he kept going. My back was cut but I struggled to get on my feet, the pain didn't matter, rage had taken over, I was going to kill him. All Service personal were unarmed in the town but most of us carried some sort of weapon, knives were common, even small Beretta pistols, but I had a cosh. They were made by the Arabs and sold very cheaply to anyone. I have one hanging in my hall at home and God help some pushy doorstep salesman.

I got to my feet and took the cosh from my pocket and charged; he turned and fled, he was running for his life and I was only a few yards behind him. Deep into the closely built adobe houses, in and out of the alleyways, it was dark and only the reflection from the white washed walls gave any kind of light. My boots made a lot of a noise when I ran over stone and dogs were barking; he was still in the lead. It was impossible to keep track among all these narrow alleys. What did he have waiting for me? I stopped dead, think man you're completely lost. I walked carefully on sand or dirt trying to keep the noise down, looking round corners trying to get a bearing and avoiding any personnel. An Arab mob could gather in seconds and that could spell big trouble for me in a place like this: I should never have chased him, I was not thinking then but now I was completely sober and all thoughts of revenge were out of my mind.

The priorities were to get out of the quarter and find the market as quietly as possible. Anyone who has been round an Arab Souk in daylight will tell you how difficult it is to negotiate and it was some time before I saw the dim oil lamps of a market. This may sound stupid but I couldn't be sure that it was the same market. I circled round the outside trying to find something familiar when I saw the three bodies: it was a shock, I thought the worst and ran over to them in trepidation.

At almost eighteen years of age I had seen a lot of death but we were on leave in a holiday situation and a pile of bodies was not on, so when I saw one move the relief was enormous. It was Woody trying to sit up. They had all been beaten with stones or clubs and one of the Fusiliers had a broken arm. When I tried to remonstrate with the watching Arabs they stood well back, it was nothing to do with them. Woody looked at me in amazement, my uniform was in tatters and I was covered in blood but I was the only one capable so it was up to me. I tried to get them on their feet but the Fusilier screamed when I touched him; I would have to get some help. I was trying to stop the traffic on the main road when two MPs in a patrol jeep saw me. I was glad that they did. When I explained the situation they couldn't do enough. They took us to hospital and for the first time I realised how badly I was cut on the back and shoulders and my backside needed stitches.

They kept the Fusilier with the broken arm in hospital and the rest of us made our way home, much wiser men. With stitches still in my backside we left for Italy a few days later. After all these years only the scars on my backside remain to remind me how stupid I could be when I tried. The leave period had been better than expected as most Battalions had only had the three days. Maybe 'They' were being compassionate because we had taken such a bashing but no sooner had we handed in our tropical kit than we were in Port Said and off to war.

The boat trip to Taranto was uneventful except for noticeable things, for example the boat had been carrying Indian troops and all the toilets had been converted to the squat type. I could never figure out why it was necessary to make these changes for other people but it was ok for us to manage; I suppose it was something to do with religion. Whilst I was using one of these squats I noticed something jammed behind a bulkhead, it was a Kukri. Every Gurkha carried one of these distinctive broad blade knives, standard issue since the 19th Century. It was some find, worth a bomb. There was no point in handing it in, the guy who lost it was long gone, so I proudly stuck it in my belt and went topside to show the lads.

We disembarked at Taranto and joined a train for the journey North. We usually travelled like cattle but this time there was rough seating, well we were winning the war. Rolling along on that northbound train I had time to think about my own position. In a few months I would be eighteen years old, the minimum age for my situation, after that the Army could say I'd left it too late to change anything. Getting out had never been a problem before, the time for me to have owned up was when I was wounded, but I didn't and now I was heading back for another dose of the same. It was nothing to do with King and Country, I had joined up for the excitement and I'd had plenty of that, so why couldn't I put my hand up? Everyone sitting in that freight truck was thinking about what happened to them last time they where here. There was no way I could take advantage and leave, I was one of the lads.

We left the train at Foggia and went west by truck to a staging area to be made up to strength. The replacements were from every outfit under the sun and we had a new Section leader. There was a wide gap between those who had seen action and those who had not. Americans were worse than us, they had Combatants and Non-combatants and there were lots of arguments between low ranking Combatants and superior Non-combatants. Our Corporal was a Non-combatant. Corporal Harker was older than anyone else and seemed a nice guy. We immediately called him Gordon, after the pre-war film star. He was ex-Artillery and had been on a course; he couldn't understand what we were laughing for.

"You saw some action in the desert then?" he asked.

"Oh yes."

He was referring to the bombing while we were thinking of something else but he wasn't one of the NCOs we had our fun with because he was going to be all right.

We headed north for the Gothic Line: it had been there when we left in February and they hadn't made much progress since. The May offensive was all about finishing off the Italian problem so that the Generals could concern themselves with Europe and opening a Second Front. The Germans were being driven north, bit by bit, but when they established a defensive position, it was a good one. The Gothic Line had been holding out for months. This was familiar territory for us and we took great delight in pointing out the gory parts of the campaign to the replacements. Patrol activity was intense on both sides but they didn't set up the old Battle Patrol method like last time, it was a case of wait your turn. When my turn came it was a patrol I will never forget.

I had not been feeling well, my urine was red, my eyes were yellow and I had a bad stomach ache. I had a bout of Jaundice when I was wounded so I knew what was wrong with me but when asked to go on patrol you can't say you don't feel like it. It was a large patrol of about twenty men and the officer who briefed us wouldn't say much.

"It's a long way so just keep up and stay quiet."

It was dark when we set off, I was feeling worse than ever and after three hours I was staggering and making

122

a lot of noise. The Sergeant kept telling me to shut up, I told him the stomach was so bad that with every jolt the pain was unbearable.

"It's just nerves, that's all."

"It's not nerves. I've been on dozens of patrols before."

To be thought 'chicken' was a very sore point with me, so the Sergeant passed the problem to the officer who looked at me and said,

"What the hell are you doing here, in such a state?"

"I didn't like to refuse sir."

"You are a bloody fool and a nuisance."

I could only agree with him.

"Well we can't go on like this. All of you wait here, I shall be back as soon as possible."

We pumped the Sergeant for more information and he told us what he knew.

Apparently we had a rendezvous with some Partisans and the less we knew the better. The Krauts had no respect for the Italians, after all they had changed sides when the going got rough but the Partisans were like the French Marquis and were treated the same, shot without mercy. That was why the officer had been so cagey; there were still a lot of Fascists working for the Germans.

"So what's now Sarg?"

"We wait here for the boss."

They sat around looking at the cause of all this bother; a kid with a Kukri stuck in his belt boasting about how many patrols he had been on. They were all new to me; none of my old mates were there to back me up but they could see I was genuinely sick. They were hoping it would all be called off and within the hour the officer returned.

"All follow me and you keep as quite as you can," and with a final gesture at me, we were off.

Half an hour later we left the road, went over a small bridge and onto a wide track. The officer posted a man on the bridge for a look out; look out for what we wondered, nobody had told us anything. A quarter of a mile along the track we came to a farmhouse with several out buildings. There were Italians about and after a lot of arm waving a woman took me inside. I followed her slowly up some stairs and she pointed at a room, it had a bed and she indicated I should make use of it. I was grateful and flopped down; there was no pain if I kept still. One of the lads came to tell me that they were having a brew up but my stomach was not up to it, so I declined. There was one amusing incident that happened whilst I lay on that bed; I would have laughed but for my stomach ache. A young Italian came into the room to look at me but before he could say anything, a signorina rushed in and started shouting at him. I could not follow all the rapid Italian but this was serious stuff, she was pleading with him not to do 'whatever'; if they had done it in song this would have been grand opera. Finally, she pulled him out of the room, neither of them taking any notice of me. I asked one of the lads what was going on to cause such a ruckus. He said the boss had sent one of the Italians to relieve the guy on the bridge so he could come in and have a brew.

"Is that all? I thought he was going to assassinate Mussolini."

"Well you know what Ities are like."

The officer gave me my next surprise; he came to tell me that they were going push off.

"We are so far behind now we won't be able to get back to you so you will have to stay here."

"For how long sir?"

"Probably tomorrow night. It's all your fault anyway."

"I thought this was the rendezvous sir."

"No it's not, we have to go on."

I realised then that I was causing more trouble than I had first thought but twenty-four hours on a soft bed helped me a lot. I had a good night's sleep and woke up in the morning to a noisy clattering in the yard outside. My stomach ache had gone and so I looked out of the window and was taken aback, the yard was full of Germans.

A raid; what to do? Hide under the bed. This child like action sounds ridiculous but if they were already in the house, I couldn't risk opening the door. No more time to think about it – move. Grabbing my rifle and pack I went under the bed. I could see the bottom of the door, if a pair of jackboots appeared, well my thinking wasn't that far advanced. I lay still and gave it some consideration. Becoming a POW sounded easy according to the German pamphlet and it was, if there were lots of you going over, but if you were on your own the risk was high. The German Commander may be in a bad mood or you may be a nuisance and interfering with a bigger plan; POWs have been shot for less.

My doleful thoughts were interrupted by the door opening and a pair of legs that didn't belong to any storm-trooper appeared in my line of sight. I moved my head out and looked up at her.
She put her finger to her lips and whispered, "Tedeschi," and indicated I should get back out of sight.
These were encouraging signs and I did as I was told.
The house went very quiet and after half an hour the signorina came to tell me the full story. It was not a raid, the Germans had stopped to brew up.
"Just like Joe's cafe on the Chester Road," I said, but she ignored my interruption. She went on to explain that there had been no trouble and some Tedeschis "do very nice mans." Her attempt at English was still better than my Italian and any doubt I had had about her ability had long gone, she was a very cool customer. The outburst I had witnessed the night before must have been love, this was business.

As soon as it got dark, a Sergeant with a small patrol came for me.
"Stomach ache all gone has it?" he said suspiciously.

"Yes Sarg, but you should have seen all the Ted's that called here."

"Yer, yer. Let's get going."

When he saw my long goodbye to the signorina, he was even more suspicious. When we got back I told the officer about the German tea break.

"I thought it might be useful intelligence sir."

He wasn't interested, all he said was, "Your eyes do look a bit funny. Go and see the MO about it."

I saw the Medical Officer and he gave me some pills and that was that; no mention in dispatches or a pat on the back, nothing.

Palmer, Woody, Yank and I were all in the same outfit and the rest of the Platoon could not understand our cavalier attitude towards the war. We constantly ribbed the Corporal but we gave him respect as well. There was one occasion when we were under fire from a building, it was a single house in the bottom corner of a field and it was the first time the Corporal had been in direct small arms fire with the enemy.

"Let's rush them," he said.

"A bayonet charge! Are you nuts, Corp?"

"It's all down hill and we'll make a lot of noise."

They all looked at us experienced types for some kind of lead. Great use was made of the bayonet in training film programmes, bully boys rushing about pulling faces and screaming. The bayonet used was always the British Lee Enfield type like the one I dropped on the Passing Out Parade in 1942 but sacks of straw don't shoot back and we had the American rifle with a bayonet like a six inch nail; it was not very impressive.

"Ok, let's do it," said Yank.

"Firing from the hip," said Palmer.

Gordon Harker was already on his feet.

"If you fire on the run, keep in a straight line or you'll shoot each other."

We all rushed down the hill screaming, firing and shouting like mad men. Four Krauts tumbled out of the front door with their hands in the air. The shooting was all over the place and they tried to keep their hands high whilst they crouched low. We stopped just in front of them, the Corporal was both pleased and amazed with himself.

"There you are, it's easy," he said.

"Don't be so sure. If these had been Paras, it would have been a different story."

We reminded him of our Battipaglia experience but he was still jubilant and said,

"Let's take them back to Company HQ."

At the Base, there were more slaps on the back for Gordon but on another occasion, he was not so happy. We were marching along a road with almost full Platoon strength with orders to keep our eyes open; Gordon was now acting as Platoon Sergeant. There were plenty of Teds in the area and the burst of machine gun fire was not unexpected; one man was hit as we scattered. There was a large house near the road and the Corporal shouted for us to take cover in there. Those of us who were close could see that the house had been badly damaged and a thick blast wall had been built across the main doorway. About half the Platoon made a mad dash for the doorway. The Corporal and I were the first, quickly joined by the others: all we could see were civilians. There was a large room; it had been cleared to make it the full size of the house. There was a staircase at the one end and the Italians crowded at the other. We all stared at each other, the Italians made the first move.

Their decision was understandable in the circumstances. Behind the crowd there was a scuffle and two German soldiers were thrown out. One of them landed at my feet; he sprawled on the tiled floor and looked up at me, he was younger than I was and terrified. He looked at me and started to beg, he was pleading for his life, which at that moment was not in any real danger. He squirmed and grovelled at my feet

127

and I was very uneasy; the other soldier said nothing. Everybody was quiet and looking at me, I looked at Gordon and he waved his arm towards the doorway, I assumed he meant chuck him out. I grabbed the kid by his shoulder harness and started to drag him out of the door. The kid saw the blast wall and went hysterical, he was in no doubt that I was going to shoot him. It was no good trying to convince him otherwise so I kept on and he grabbed frantically at the floor.

These young soldiers were told they could expect no mercy if they were caught and the propaganda seemed to work if this kid was an example. The rest of the Platoon had joined us and now I had quite an audience. The wounded man was getting all the Corporal's attention, so while he bandaged the man's arm, I had to deal with the screaming kid. I shouldered my rifle so I could use two hands on his shoulder harness, I was so intent on getting him through the door that I didn't notice how exposed I was between the blast wall and the house. If the burst of fire had been a foot lower it would have killed us both. As the bullets ricocheted off the wall, I let go of the Kraut and dashed inside. The others had already made for the top of the house.

At the top of the stairs, apart from a small landing, the room had been cleared the same as below except for a stone sink with a tap. It must have been used for some kind of HQ. There had been large windows but the glass and frames had long gone. Yank went over to one of them and foolishly leaned out; it was a miracle that he survived as shots came from all directions and one hit his helmet.
He stumbled back into the centre and shouted, "There's dozens of them all round the place."
One of the lads, a tall chap called Lofty, contorted himself trying to get under the sink. We didn't smile; we would laugh later, if there was a later. Yank, who was sitting on the floor still dazed from the blow on his

helmet, suddenly shouted,

"Shut up and listen."

We did just that and what we heard was the unmistakable squeak, squeak and crunch of a tank.

"They are going to crush the house on us."

"What about the Ities?"

"They won't give a damn about them."

Gordon looked round at all our faces and said.

"I think its hands up time lads," and made for the stairs. Most of the Platoon was halfway down the stairs when I shouted,

"Wait," they looked up at me for an explanation.

"What about the two Teds?"

"What about them?" Gordon was looking very anxious.

"Right now one of them is telling his Sergeant that I was going to shoot him against the wall."

"Well you weren't were you?"

"No but I never had time to make that clear, did I?"

The more I thought about this the worse it seemed. I know how I would have behaved if I had been in the kid's position.

"The Ities will back us up, they saw everything."

"I can't rely on the Italians. Look how they shopped the two Teds. They would do the same to me."

"I'm sorry Golly, we have no choice."

There was nodding agreement with the Corporal and I had no idea what was my best move. Yank who was still in the centre of the room made a comment, I turned to look, he was standing up staring out of the window. When he shouted the words, it was like a shot to the nervous system.

"It's a Sherman."

They all came back into the room to check for themselves; this changed everything.

"He's right, it's a bloody Sherman."

On the same road and from the same direction that we had come was a beautiful Sherman Tank.

"Attract his attention," shouted Gordon.

Keeping well back from the windows we jumped up

and down waving our arms to no avail.

"Fire at him," suggested someone and without considering the consequences or who had said it, we blasted away bouncing bullets off the armoured turret. The Tank stopped and its gun swung to face us.

"Jesus Christ, stop shooting and wave."

The Corporal took up the lead again and we made a desperate effort to attract attention getting closer to the windows. The Tank opened fire with its machine gun and we all hit the floor before we realised that the fire was directed at the lower part of the house. As we ventured near the windows, we could see the Tank was well in control. The Germans had scattered and we leaned out of the windows and made it clear who we were. Later we went over to the Tank and a Sergeant stuck his head out and said,

"What the hell are you God damn Limeys playing at; I thought we were on the same side."

"It was the only way to get your attention. Did we do any damage?"

"You owe us a paint job."

The Sergeant was a great guy and when we told him that we thought he was a German Tiger tank he said,

"If there's any Tigers around you won't see my arse for dust."

Everyone knew that on a one to one, the Sherman was no match for a Tiger. He offered to give us a lift but we declined. Infantry, as a general rule, didn't like Tanks; they drew heavy fire and the infantryman was vulnerable to any weapon from bow and arrows upwards. This time we were glad to make their acquaintance and a ride on a tank would be very nice but nevertheless we watched the Sherman roll away. We followed in the way we new best, along the road always looking for a deep ditch just in case of the odd surprise.

After our spell in Egypt, there seemed to be some

doubt about what to do with us; were we staying with the American 5th Army or not? Not that it matters to the rank and file, dying is the same whatever badge you're wearing. It was after the war when I found out the reason for all the uncertainty. Back home all the talk was about opening a Second Front in Europe and Italy was out of the news, but they forgot that Cassino still had to be taken and what about Rome? These places had hogged the headlines for months so they still had to be dealt with.

Not to be left out of the chaos, Mother Nature joined in and the volcano Vesuvius blew its top and showered us with ash, pumice and soot. You could always depend on the poor bloody infantry to come up with something so we had an outbreak of scabies.

Our Medical Officer was a good 'un; not only did he have to decide who was a genuine shellshock victim, and some guys could be good actors when things got desperate, but he also took time to explain how to avoid being bitten by Black Widow spiders, deal with a dose of clap and now dozens of men going down with scabies. Scabies are tiny insects that breed under the skin and are very infectious. The MO sent people away for treatment and when they came back they were painted purple. Yank was sharing a tent with me and he caught it but I didn't. I don't understand why, my experience with the infection came months later. Yank went away for treatment and never returned, we never found out why but we all missed him. He was quick on the draw with his .45 and great fun to have around whether he was a phoney or not it didn't matter, he was our mate.

After one of the bloodiest battles of the war, the Poles finally took Cassino and we were no longer wanted in that sector, so they moved us north. As we drove along the coast road the sky was lit up with the brilliant firework display of Vesuvius' eruptions and our vehicle was covered by fine soot from the fallout.

Chapter 13

The Not So Holy City

Bivouacked somewhere south of Rome we took it easy. It was not always possible to stay with a mate, bivouacking in the dark or under shell fire you had to take pot luck, sort it out later was the way. If you were going to move in a few hours, it wasn't worth the bother of changing around, which is why I was stuck with Pittaway, a little man with a temper.

All over Italy women were selling their bodies to make ends meet. This was a war thing or a refugee problem, call it what you may but for thousands of years all over the world, whenever a Country is occupied by an invader, it happens. People who live in a Country that has never had the experience shouldn't pass judgment. Women were after money, food, blankets or anything so it was no surprise to me to be called from behind a wall by a girl. I went over to check; she was about nineteen and she had an old pram that was full of army food. My bivouac was close to the wall, I looked round, nobody was paying attention, so I made a quick decision. If she was seen by some of the men they would take all her stuff away so I decided to help her and myself. The dry stone wall was down in places, so I gestured to her to move along to a gap. I put some loose stones round the pram so it wouldn't be too obvious and pointed to my bivouac.
She hesitated, "You food?"
"No, money," says I.
"Ok Joe."

She'd done a bit of business around the Yanks. Half covering her with my leather jerkin we hurried to the tent. Once inside, I couldn't concentrate on the sex, my mind was on the commercial possibility on offer. Economics suggested fifty Lira for ten minutes.

Seventy five percent of the men would be interested. While I was dreaming of being rich, Pittaway stuck his head in.

"God, what a stink. I'm not having this." He then stood outside the tent and shouted, "Darlington's got a dirty little whore in here."

I was outside in a flash; I shook the little bugger and screamed in his face,

"She's not a dirty whore, she's just a kid trying to make her way like the flash birds in Naples."

"She stinks." I wasn't having it.

"No worse than you and me at the moment."

By now we had attracted too much attention. Heads were popping out all over the field so I told the girl to get away quickly. She pointed to the others who were making their way to our tent, no doubt thinking of all that business, but this shambles was no good to me. I made out that officers would be here soon and would harangue her and make trouble. She understood that all right and made off. Pittaway then held court telling his version and all the guys were looking at me like I was an insect. That was not the only time I had a shindig with Pittaway.

We bivouacked again in another area, a few miles nearer to Rome and set up a regular camp with the other two Companies in nearby fields. All the talk was about the anticipated attack on the Capital. Unbeknown to us of course, it was the argument about who was going to be first into the City. General Clark claimed the privilege for the Americans and we were still part of his outfit as far as we knew. All that this meant to us was a lot of hanging about and with nothing better to do I got blind drunk, fell and did my ankle in. The MO thought it was broken and sent me to a Forward Dressing Station. They kept me for two days, strapped up the ankle and sent me back. When I arrived at the camp, it was deserted but there was Pittaway walking up and down between the lines carrying a baseball bat.

"They're on special manoeuvres, won't be back till tomorrow, I've got to stop any pilfering."
"Good, I'll go and find some grub then."
I went into the cook tent and found some meat. Now I knew a little about field kitchens so I tried to set up the system. Banger Jackson had no trouble when he did it; the trick was to get a tin with a small hole in it to drip oil onto a metal strip that ran into a little fire that flared up with a hot flame every few seconds, easy. I had the fire going and was working on the tin of oil when Pittaway showed up.
"What are you doing with that?"
"I'm trying to cook some grub."
"My orders are to stop anybody touching anything."
"They mean the kids not us, now piss off or I won't give you any when I've done."
"No, you must put all that stuff back," he swung the club to make his point.
"I'll stick that up your arse if you don't let me get on."

I have to say Pittaway had a lot of guts and he went for me, but it was too late I was already on my feet. I took the club off him easily and waltzed him round the fire. He was still throwing punches at me so I gave him a push and he tripped over, unfortunately knocking the oil over. The oil splashed all over his trousers before it ignited, he rushed off between the tents screaming. I had to get him down and smother the flames; I grabbed a canvas fly-sheet and went after him, my bandaged ankle wasn't any help but I managed to get him down. When I lifted the canvas, I could see that the bottoms of his trousers were too burned to pull away from the skin. Wrapping the canvas tight round both legs I told him to lie still while I got some help. The other Company was not on the field exercise so I ran over and got their Medics to come back with me. The last I saw of Pittaway was when they put him on the stretcher; then I picked up the base ball bat and walked up and down the tent lines, wondering what I was going to tell the others, when they could see there had been some unofficial changes made.

I don't know what happened to Pittaway but I did hear a rumour that he came back to the mob, made Corporal and got the Military Medal for some daring-do but I was never able to confirm this when I checked at the Military Museum in London. To Pittaway I can only say I'm sorry old son and that after you left I cleaned up the cook tent and didn't try to use Banger Jackson's equipment again.

Rome fell two days before the Normandy landing in Europe, so it disappeared from the headlines before anyone could get used to it. I hope it was made clear to the troops in the D-Day invasion that it had all been done before in Sicily and Italy and they were benefiting from lessons we had learned a year before. The fall of Rome was a damp squib as far as the poor bloody infantry was concerned. There had been talk of another Stalingrad; the truth was that Rome had been declared an open City. We marched in and the Germans marched out; the Pope had done another of his side deals. There was little damage in the City; it must have been annoying to both Berliner and Londoner to see how some cities got away with it.

Some officers always assumed that other ranks were morons and one of these officers explained about the Coliseum.
"These ruins are nothing to do with us, they've always looked like that."
"They didn't look like that in Nero's time sir. It was a going concern then, like Hatton Garden."
"All right Darlington, you've made your point, now shut up."

In the evening the Coliseum was still very much a going concern; every arch had a prostitute working

135

there like a galley slave for less than a price of a packet of cigarettes.

There was some good news though; we were going back to Rome for a victory cavalcade and a blessing by the Pope. When Caesar's Roman Legions entered the city after a successful campaign, like conquering Britain for instance, they came to the city for accolades and praise. Their leaders would kill a few prisoners for show; it's much the same now except it's more civilized. Now the leaders are elected to Congress or get a knighthood, the rest of us get a "Well done, lads."

Now that we were entering for a victory parade, the prices would stabilise and the girls would not be giving it away for a packet of cigarettes anymore. We assembled at some back streets near to St Peter's, ready for the Pope's blessing. There was a little more leeway at this point and Catholics could join a parade and march into St Peter's Square. The rest of us were not exactly told to clear off and do as we like but that is what we did. Woody was a little concerned
"Maybe we should have gone and got the Pope's blessing."
"Why, what difference would it make?"
"Well, you used to go to church on Sundays."
"Yes, but only to get a cup of tea and a free bun."
"You didn't believe it all then?"
"No of course not and what's more, that Pope was blessing Germans only two weeks ago."
Woody was persistent, "That means he's not taking sides."
"That means he's hedging his bets and not doing anything."
I was never going to be convinced.
Fifty years later, the Church publicly acknowledged its duplicity during the war years.

It was very rare for us to hear a civilian radio but when

we did it was still pumping out propaganda news by Axis Sally, she even mentioned the Black Cats which made us feel very important. Another of her favourite tricks was trying to upset the Yanks by making out they were the lackeys of the British like the old colonial days. Her signature tune was Between the Devil and the Deep Blue Sea, very apt.

Stuff was pouring in from Anzio; they had had a very tough time after we had left but now it was the most useful port in all of Italy, only twenty miles south of the Eternal City and it was proving its worth. I just hope those Generals thought it was worth the blood bath when they collected their medals….

We wandered about the Vatican without a plan and missed the most interesting things, which is the way it is with uneducated soldiers. I cannot say too much on this subject without reminding myself of my own shortcomings. I personally regret it because Roman history was a favourite of mine and the opportunity was lost forever.

When all the pomp and protocol was over we got into our designated vehicles and were taken to a large transit camp where the restructuring of our battered Battalion continued. Although the Italian campaign no longer existed according to the News, we still had a large part of Italy to conquer, so there was more dying to do and one death I remember well. We moved to the mountainous area in central Italy and were soon on the offensive.

Our objective was a small monastery, nothing grand like Monte Cassino. Nothing to worry about, said an Intelligence Officer who came to brief us, only lightly defended and maybe the Teds had scarpered already. The only problem, there was no road, we'd have to climb up to it. This from a man who had never climbed anything higher than a jeep. They put together a mob of strangers, remains of other units that had suffered casualties the same as we had and made it up to Battalion strength; but there was no esprit de corps in this outfit, not like the old Ox and Bucks. The battle plan was: A Company to climb the north side, C Company the South and B Company in reserve.

We started in the morning and the weather was fine. You could not see the monastery from the foot of the mountain and our orders were, "keep going up". I was in A Company and our Platoon took the lead. The climb was strenuous but we didn't need ropes, we always followed the one who found the easy route and we started to straggle into single file. We climbed steadily for an hour with the Corporal and I jockeying for position. We all got to like Corporal Harker; he was one of us and didn't mind us calling him Gordon. I was climbing like a monkey and got ahead,
"Come on Gordon keep up."

While I could still hear remarks like, "Cheeky young bugger," I pulled myself up to shoulder height and what I saw stopped my heart. On a ledge several feet wide sat two Germans with a Spandau machine gun pointing straight into my face. My mind was not in a fit state to make rational judgments or I would have asked myself why the Krauts hadn't made a move. When they heard us climbing up, we were in such a vulnerable position a hand grenade thrown over the edge would have seen us off. The seconds seemed like hours as we stared at each other.

The Corporal below was impatient, "What's the matter, get a move on."
Without looking down I shouted, "Shut up."
My snap command jerked the two Teds into action and they put their hands up and my heart started up again. I pulled myself over the edge and crawled towards them, still expecting a kick in the face but all was well and I sat between them with a sigh of relief.

The position was well made; the rock had been cut back to make a large platform and a lot of man hours had been put into setting this up. If this was a sample of their fortifications, they were not going to be a push over.

I joked with the two Teds, they smiled and said, "Camerad, camerad," and of course I agreed with them. I was now ready for the Corporal.
"C'mon Gordon, get a move on, what you playing at."
His head appeared over the edge. His astonishment was worse than mine had been, but at least there was one friendly face to greet him.
"C'mon Corp, we're all mates here." I gave the Teds a slap on their shoulders,
"Ya, Ya, camerad," they both chorused.
"What do we do now?" He gasped, his eyes and chin level with the rock.
"We can't keep talking to the top of your head, come and join us."
The Corporal still hesitating said, "That one's got a grenade in his boot," he tried to talk without drawing attention to what he was saying.

I didn't think there was any need to be coy, so I turned to the German. He did have a stick grenade stuck in the top of his jackboot so I just pointed and indicated for him to hand it over. He did with a smile but as the Corporal saw the movement, he dropped out of sight.
"C'mon Corp, come and have a rest." Gordon's head appeared again.
"Jesus Christ Golly, stop pissing about."
Just as he was pulling himself over, there was some machine gun fire nearby and he dropped out of sight again. I shouted down to him,
"It's ok, it's probably C Company in trouble. Tell them we are sending two Teds down and they will be no bother."
When Gordon came on the ledge again he wandered to the far end and came back all excited.

"You can see the monastery from there. Let's rest up and let them tell us what they want to do."

"I've been trying to get you to do that for the last ten minutes."

I lay back and put my feet up on the machine gun barrel and waited; somebody would come along and muck us about and sure enough, it wasn't long before an officer came up looking for trouble.

"You two responsible for those two Krauts?"

"Yes sir."

"So what's going on now?"

"If you stand at that end, you can see the monastery. We didn't know what to do about it sir."

"You keep going, that's what."

I had the feeling that this was not a well planned operation and my instinct had kept me alive before. We moved with caution; the ledge was already too crowded so we got going and it was easy now the mountain had levelled out. As more of the Company approached, everyone got less cautious; it appeared that the building was uninhabited and there were no windows or doors on the side we were looking at. There were slit trenches cut into the rock about thirty yards from the base of the wall. Gordon and I were uneasy and we told the rest of the Platoon. Most of the lads wandering around didn't know about the two machine gunners we had caught.

"They wouldn't have been sent out there for fun," said Gordon and I agreed.

"Maybe those shots we heard were a signal."

Nobody seemed to be bothered and it was decided to wait until we were at full strength before trying to enter the monastery. There was something creepy about this quiet building and I didn't think the Officer-in-Charge had a clue what to do. Gordon gave orders for the Platoon to stay in or near the cut outs in the rock. Woody and I sat on the edge of a trench smoking, we were all waiting for C Company. Late in the day C Company joined us, they had had a harder climb than us, so we waited while they sorted themselves out. There was now a mob of over fifty men milling around the thirty foot walls, it was lunacy.

The Germans appeared on top of the walls with armfuls of grenades throwing them at random, causing maximum panic with everyone rushing to get into already crowded trenches. The casualties were enormous; our Corporal was one of them; Woody and I witnessed the whole scene. The Corporal stood for a second looking to see which trench was nearest when the grenade landed by his side: he disappeared before our very eyes; Corporal V. Harker 1764557, 7th Battalion Oxfordshire and Buckinghamshire Light Infantry, was gone.

The reason I know his initial and number is because the War Office, operating from the Blue Coat School in Liverpool, sent me a letter on 13th March 1945 asking what had happened to him; I still have the letter. Apparently no one had collected the dog tag or reported his death, which is not surprising given the circumstances at the time. We never knew what the V stood for, he was always Gordon to us.

At last, the panic was under control. Once we had a few people in firing positions we could keep the Teds off the wall and the grenades stopped except for the odd one that got lobed over by a German that kept out of sight which fell harmlessly close to the wall. We couldn't throw grenades back as the walls were too high and when it was tried, they fell back on our side. We needed a two-inch mortar but no one had thought of that, it was basic incompetence. Clearing up after the carnage, moving the dead and sending the wounded down the mountain took time and it was dusk before we had some sort of order. C Company, on the other side of the building, were in no better shape. What were we doing in this hopeless position? The monastery could have been knocked out by an air strike, but I suppose we didn't rate any priority. A Girl Guide troop armed with sticks could have defended the fortress because our position was so vulnerable. All they could tell us, as it started to get dark was, "Find a good defensive position and wait."

In other words, nobody knew what to do but the Germans did and in the middle of the night, they did it. If only the monastery had been illuminated, the Krauts couldn't have come out of the dark the way they did. The mystery was where had they come from; there were no windows or doors on our side, they must have crept silently along the foot of the wall and lined up in front of us. They came at us in mass, screaming, firing automatic weapons and throwing grenades. According to intelligence this place was lightly defended, what a farce! We were overwhelmed and we ran; to a man we ran and I'm not afraid to admit that I ran as fast as anyone. It took time to get up this mountain but on the way down, I just jumped into the blackness, it didn't matter if it was two feet or two hundred feet, anything to get away from the murderous fire. At daybreak I looked for Woody and when I found him he was in the same state as me, battered and bloody. There were other groups of men wandering about, no officers could be found and the NCOs were no help, it was still a case of every man for himself. Woody and I decided to stick together and make our own way. We kept close to the hedgerows ready to duck out of sight if we heard any German. We moved in what we assumed to be a southerly direction and made slow progress, my partners legs were in a bad condition.

Once we heard a rumour that we were going home,
Back to dear old Blighty, never more to roam,
Then someone said, "In France you'll fight,"
We answered, "No, we'll just sit tight,"
The windy D-Day Dodgers, in sunny Italy.

Chapter 14

I could always get a job as a milkmaid

Having decided to spend that night in a ruined farm and to make an early start in the morning, finding food and sorting ourselves out would be our first priority. Exactly where, we were would have to wait until we found some military signs. When we made our move at first light we were feeling more decisive, so at the first farm we saw with signs of habitation we went for broke. As we approached an old guy came out, we only had one rifle between us and Woody waved it with menace.

"Dove il Tedeshi."
The old guy ran back into the house.
"Use your head," I said, "it's no good getting tough, we need food and information."
I took the rifle off him and walked into the farmhouse with it on my shoulder, the old guy had been joined by his wife and they both stared at me; they were both very frightened.
"Bongerno, multi beni casa," I said with a smile, "Quanto da qui alla Tedeshi." I needed to know if there were any near by.
"No Tedeshi, no Tedeshi."
The old girl was pointing her arms in all directions, she thought we would behave like the Germans if we found the enemy on the premises. Little did she know that we didn't know what we were doing.
"Dove Inglese." The old lady went to the window and pointed, "Inglese, Inglese."
I pointed to another track and tried again. "Dove conduce questa strada."
Woody was very impressed when she insisted that the English were down there as well.
"We're in the clear then son, now try and get some grub."

"We're not sorted yet, she's telling me what I want to hear, she's smarter than the old man."

"Mota appertito," I said pointing to my mouth.

"Si, Si."

The old man got that and went out of the room, returning with bread and cheese. While I had the old man's attention, I made signs with my hands for something to drink. He hesitated, probably worried that I would pinch all his best Vermouth. His wife came to the rescue,

"Momento, momento," she left the room. I was still a bit suspicious so I followed her but she was only going to milk the cow. I watched her and she let me have a go, I was very pleased with my new skill and I took Arthur a mug full.

"It's warm," he said.

"Of course it is, this is your genuine stuff not your bottled rubbish."

It seemed a good time to make tracks again and I'm sure that the old couple were glad to see us go. It was still early morning but after about an hour we heard voices. We were careful not to show ourselves until we were sure they were English. There was a group of squaddies having an augment. Two Corporals came to us.

"Are you B Company?"

"No."

"Where are they?"

"No idea."

"We've got a Sergeant with us who's gone off his head. The guys want to bump him off before he gets us all killed."

"If we had been Ted, we could have done all of you, the row you were making," said Woody.

"That's the problem, we can't keep the nutter quiet." The Corporal was a very worried man and went on,

"We're all C Company. He's not one of ours and the lads are very jumpy after what happened up there."

"We all took a hammering but bumping him off is a bit

drastic isn't it?" asked Woody.

"Let me have a go," I said and walked over to the group.

"Left, right, quick march, stand still, by the left," the Sergeant was shouting.

The lads stood round; if anyone had made a first move, they would have been on him like a pack of Wolves. I indicated to them to let me have some room then touched the madman on the back; he turned round and although I didn't recognise him he was clearly deranged.

"Come up that man there."

I stood to attention and shouted, "Sergeant, the men are waiting for you over there." I pointed to the field.

"My men, my men. About turn."

I went and stood in a gap in the hedge, "Sergeant they're here."

I moved into the field and he followed me. There were some trees about a quarter of a mile away.

"Your men are waiting there for your orders Sergeant." I pointed at the trees.

"I see them, I see them."

I was glad he thought he could see them because my plan was to knock him unconscious if all else failed.

"Quickly, we must go to them," and I started to run. I looked back, he was running fast as he past me.

I said, "Go Sergeant, I'll try to keep up."

I sat on the grass and watched him go, shouting, "As you were, as you were."

I ran back to the lads waiting in the road. "We had better clear off before he comes back."

Woody said, "You've just saved that bomb happy sod's life."

Maybe, I thought, "But who knows where he'll finish up!"

Woody made light of it by saying, "If he gets to that farmhouse, she'll give him a mug of warm milk." The Corporals congratulated me for solving their problem.

None of us knew at that time that thirty years later I

would use the same trick when one of my employees went berserk in the factory and tried to kill the foreman. The nurse was to terrified to go near the man but I talked him into the office where two men from the Asylum grabbed him and took him away in a white van; but let's get back to the war.

We spilt up into two groups, each with a Corporal in charge. We set off down the road but only the first group was armed, all the others had lost their weapons. I was with the first lot and it was late in the afternoon before we saw two Red Caps sitting in a jeep at a crossroads.
"We'll be all right now Corp. Those bastards won't be within five miles of the front line."
I said this with a certain amount of bitterness and when Woody caught up with us he said the same thing.
"Are you two twins or something?" said the Corporal.
"No but we've done a bit in the last ten months."
The Corporal stared, "Were you in the original landings then?"
"Yes and they've already done us once, so we're extra careful."
"Who did, the red caps or the Krauts?"
"Both."
We crowded around the two cops, who didn't seem at all surprised to see us,
"We've been gathering you lot up for the last twenty four hours. You're all over the place."

It was no good explaining to these types the reason why, so we let them tell us where to go next and we finally reached an assembly point. We were put in the 2nd/5th Queen's, a famous Regiment that we knew nothing about, so now our new title was C Company, 2nd/5th Queen's Mediterranean Forces, Italy. There were still familiar faces about so we made the best of our new home.

I had an unusual encounter when we were on the march outside Rome. We were all spread out in single file when suddenly an old crone attacked me scratching, spitting and screaming. I held her off as best I could whilst the others stood around laughing. I had to get rough to extract myself from the old cow and we moved on; I thought no more about it. A few days later in the Stars and Stripes, there was her picture. The Stars and Stripes was a newspaper issued by the Americans and we read it whenever we got the chance. The 'old crone' was only nineteen years old and she had seen her family massacred in the Ardeatine Caves. The story went on to say how she had gone mad and was attacking anyone in uniform; I had thought that she was at least eighty. That was the first time any of us had heard of the Caves. There was plenty said about it after the War at the Nuremberg War Trials. The Germans carried out the atrocity as a reprisal because they were having trouble with the Italians before they evacuated Rome.

German atrocities were not our concern, unless it affected us directly. They had to try and kill us and visa versa and some nasty things were done in the heat of the moment. The average infantryman had an affection for his opposite number, not always understood by the superiors of either side.

Some people would call looting an atrocity but I took the view that if you were in an enemy country it was ok. If any of our own people took advantage to loot during the bombing back home, they should have been shot; that was a completely different matter. Most of us were building up a cache of loot now we were back in action and I had a grand opportunity in a mansion house not far from Rome. It was a large ornate building and apart from the damage we had done to it in getting the Germans out, it was in first class condition. This place had money written all over it, perhaps a big wig in the Fascist Party or a Count's home; we had had quite a nervous time in getting this far and were in no hurry to get out and press on. Most of the lads made for the wine cellars but I went upstairs.

There were some squaddies looking in the rooms. I went into one and there were two guys each end of a dressing table staring at a jewel box.
"It's too obvious, it's got to be a booby," they were nodding in agreement.
"Give it a poke with your rifle," said one.
"No, too risky. I'm out of here," said the other.
That left me with the decision, I shut my eyes tight and snatched it up; closing my eyes would have made no difference if it had been a booby-trap. I opened the box and there was nothing in the beautiful satin lined upholstery, the pearls were gone. I'm sure that it had contained pearls as the impression was clear. I threw the box at the other two guys who where looking round the door.
"I wouldn't have shared them with you anyway," I said with antagonism.
I decided to search thoroughly and looked in cupboards and wardrobes and there in a trunk was an evening suit laid out in tissue paper. I've always admired evening dress, so I removed my webbing and jacket and tried on the coat, it was a perfect fit, and it even had tails. I didn't mix with the right kind of society for evening dress, so I wasn't sure about this. I went out of the room for other opinions.
"Cor' blimey, it's Fred Astaire!" They all took the piss but Woody agreed that Fred always wore one.
"I've seen lots of his movies and you can cut the tails off." It was ridiculous but I couldn't see it and I decided to keep it, I folded it up and put it in a sand bag. I was going to send it home.

We moved to Central Italy and the weather got worse. There was no relief and no chance for me to deal with my prize; my sand bag was now a sodden mess. While

I was wading across a small river with the water up to my chest, I stumbled and trying to hold onto my Fred Astaire outfit made matters much worse so I threw it into the centre of the river in disgust. I watched it sail away from me with regret; what could I have been thinking of, a posh evening suit in the middle of all this filth, I must be losing my mind.

In the months that followed the invasion of Europe in June, the Italian war was no longer news worthy. We were completely ignored and yet we were about to face some of the worst battles of the campaign. The German stratagem was to retreat slowly and form a series of strong defensive positions. The Gustav Line, which included Cassino had taken months to crack: there was the Caesar Line, the Hitler Line and even the Albert Line. I would have had a few laughs with that one if I had been involved but for now it was the Gothic Line and we were in for a pasting.

From what I learned about the Italian war, when information was available, there had never been a master plan. It was thought that the Germans would abandon the Country as soon as we invaded yet there we were, ten months later and having only advanced one hundred and fifty miles as the crow flies but a thousand miles as the PBI walks.

The next major town north was Bologna but before that there were numerous villages and farms so it was house to house and very scary. Woody trod on an antipersonnel mine; it jumped out of the ground but the second explosion failed to go off. You are supposed to throw yourself flat on the ground as soon as you hear the first bang: the mine jumps about six feet into the air, then the main explosion blows your head off. It fell between us but neither of us had reacted quickly enough. Training is one thing, reality is quite another. It happened to other people in that same field; the mines had either been sabotaged or badly laid. Either way we lay there in shock for some time. If the mines had been sabotaged at the factory in Germany by slave workers, then they had our undying gratitude in the true sense of the phrase.

At another farm two of us were detailed to check out a barn, I ran forward with a Scotsman; we agreed to meet on the other side and went in opposite directions round the building. I got to the back but there was no sign of Jock. I carried on to the next corner and saw him crouched down near the end of the wall. When I got close to him, I could see that he was dead. I checked his body but there were no wounds; his face was very grey like he had been dead for some time but it had only been minutes. There were no windows on the lower part of the building so I still couldn't tell if it was occupied I sat very still by the body and listened but there was too much noise around.

We carried hand grenades on our person wherever we could. If your ammunition pouches were empty then you put them in there but the favourite was the gas mask case: get rid of the mask and fill the bag with grenades. I sat next to Jock and made a decision and although he was past caring, I moved away out of respect. I was not going to risk going round the building again throwing grenades at the upper windows so I moved along the wall until I could see a window with all the frame missing. I opened my gas mask case took out one grenade, pulled the pin and still holding on to the lever, put my hand back in the bag; there should have been at least four more in there. I stood up into a good throwing position, let go of the lever and threw whole case full through the window, then ran like hell. Four seconds later the whole wall came down. The officer wanted to know what was going on.
"Jock bought it sir."
"What do you mean? How?"
"It must have been blast, there were no wounds on him sir."

"Did you get his dog tags?"

"No sir, I forgot."

"Well go back and get them then, you bloody fool."

The invasion of Italy was two fold. The British 8th Army landed in the Gulf of Taranto and the American 5th Army landed in the Gulf of Salerno. When the 8th Army, advancing along from the south, caught up with the 5th there was bound to be some overlap. Although nobody made it clear to us, it appeared that we were now part of the British 8th Army. Why the American 5th Army didn't want us anymore was not up for discussion. In any case, it made not the slightest bit of difference to the infantryman's lot; mud is the same whatever army he his in. Maybe we changed Armies because there were more mountains and rivers on the East coast and the plains north of Rome would have been too easy for us!

The casualties were mounting now. Clearing villages with civilians still in them is not something you forget. I saw a dead mother lying in the road with a crying three year old child sitting by her body. The sort of picture that in later wars would be taken by some photographer and sent around the world causing horror and disgust on our television screens; but I just ran past her to the next house. We had no cards with rules of engagement on them and neither did the enemy; when there were civilians in the same room as German soldiers, we still threw the grenades in regardless of the inevitable consequences. We did not have the luxury of being able to stand and agonise over the morality of such actions; had we done so we would have been machine gunned down by the enemy. That is how war is. Today's scrutiny of battlefield actions is conducted from the safety of a comfortable armchair rather than actual context of the bullet filled air of the killing fields. I am sorry that my language is pedestrian but I haven't the words to make it sound any better.

At this bad time we had another shock, Palmer turned up with a stripe on his arm; he hadn't had time to sew it on properly, it was on an armband.

"I thought we all agreed not to accept any promotion?" I said.

All the original gang were given the same opportunity, so we were quite rough with him.

"They kept on to me so I said ok but I won't give you lot any orders."

"We won't take any notice of you if you do," we chorused.

The remainder of the old Platoon was a very close bunch because of what we had been through and we took this breach of faith very seriously. Anyway, Palmer, the unpaid acting Lance Corporal, was now an outcast.

A few days later we were in single file marching up a road, using the drainage ditch to keep low when Palmer, who was about six men ahead of me, shouted,

"What are we sloshing about in all this shit for, there's nothing about?"

With that, he climbed onto the bank: there was a single shot. We all crouched down and waited for the order to get moving. When I reached Palmer, he was lying head down the bank. The single shot had hit him on the bridge of his nose and his spectacles had fallen on each side of his face, still on his ears: it was either a perfect sniper's shot or a fluke. I stood staring at the body while the other guys moved past.

I was still there when Woody caught up and said,

"Poor sod, he never had a chance to give any orders."

"No and he never had a chance to show us his driving skill either," I replied.

"Get moving," said a voice of authority, "you're holding up the column."

We moved on, each with our own private thoughts on the unfortunate Palmer.

In the August of 1944 we were different people to the young boys of 1942 and well aware of our luck in still being around but the odds were shortening all the time.

The push north became more hazardous and we were pinned down on the defensive more than was being reported. The European mainland campaign was going well and nobody wanted to hear bad news, like us. We were on what was known as the Gothic Offensive but Gothic Defensive would have been more correct.

In writing this story, I have had some difficulty with names and dates but one name that sticks is Montefiore. It was sometime in August, my 18th birthday had been and gone without me being aware of it. I was now old enough to be doing all the things a war gives you license to do. The fact that I had been doing it for the last two years was beside the point. I was now legitimate, how many eighteen year olds could say that?

We had been under heavy bombardment for hours so we were well dug in when our Platoon was told to go forward up the slope. The group was nearly a mile up the slope and still not at the top when nevertheless, the order to dig in was given and we made a half-hearted attempt to scrape ourselves into the ground. It is difficult to dig a trench when lying on your face but when the Germans started using rockets, it was "get your head down" time. Multi-barrelled Nebelwefers were their favourite or 'moaning minis', as we called them. During a quiet moment the Company Commander joined us but he was without his runner. Usually the officer's batman acted as his runner when the officer was in action but this time the CO was alone. It was a pitch black night, the only illumination was from shell bursts and flares. Crawling about in the dark the CO had come to a decision.

"What's your name?" I was the nearest so I answered him,
"Darlington, sir."
"Right, I want you to go back there and get the rest of the Company up here."

Go back there could mean anywhere but it was no good trying to discuss the object of the question, so I crawled along the ground and took my place next to Woody. I whispered in Woody's ear,
"With a bit of luck he might share his fags with you," then I was off down the hill.

I jogged down the grass slope; it was full of shell holes and in the darkness I went sprawling several times. I had to get down flat when the sky lit up because a lone figure out here would be popped by both sides. I found some vacant slit trenches, they'd had a bigger pasting here from the rockets than we had had up the hill. They were not going to be easy to find and you had to be careful about passwords.

Passwords were a joke most of the time but not under these circumstances, if someone shouted, "What colour are Nell's knickers?" the wrong answer would be followed by a burst of machine gun fire. I can't remember what the idiotic sign was for that night but I must have got it right because I found someone who put me on the right track and eventually I confronted the officer the CO had told me to find.
"The Company Commander would like you to bring the rest of the Company up the hill to join him, sir."
It was so dark we could barely see each other; the voices came out of the blackness from all around.
"Tell him to fuck off sir, we've done our whack."
The Officer was very concerned but it was not a direct order so he made his own judgment.
"You can see how it is, I can't ask any more of these men tonight."
"So what shall I do, sir?"

"Do what these men have requested and fuck off."
They had made it perfectly clear I was not wanted but at the same time I was in no hurry to get back to the foreword group, so with the exchange of a few expletives, for which the British soldier is famous, I left and made my way up the slope. I thought that as long as I went up the hill it would be all right but it took too long, I had completely lost my bearings and I was lost. I have since been to the area round Gemmano on holiday and on a nice sunny day with a glass of wine in your hand it is hard to see what the problem was but on a black night in 1944 and totally lost, I could have been anywhere.

Then I heard voices but the relief turned off instantly as I recognised the guttural sound of German. I was down on my face in a second, hoping that no flares would go up. By turning my head I could make out silhouettes of the Teds' helmets bobbing up and down against the skyline at the top of the hill, they were digging in. An inch at a time I slid backwards down the grass; it would be a long time before I would risk getting up and making a run so I decided to stay on the slope and make my way to the left. I was moving so cautiously it would be daylight before I sorted myself out but caught out here, both sides would take a pop at me. When I heard English voices I was flat on my face again, they were below me. I had gone too high up the hill in the first place. I had to think carefully now because I was coming onto them from the wrong direction and they would be very trigger-happy.

I called out the password and moved quickly from the spot; there was no firing so I called out again and we made contact.
"Where's the rest of the patrol?" they asked.
"There isn't one, I'm on my own. Where's the CO?"
"Dunno, I think he's gone down. The Sergeant's about."
What a shambles I thought; I'll have to go down the

hill and start all over again. I joined up with Woody who had got the trench quite a lot deeper.

"That's a good idea Arthur, get it as deep as you can. The Teds are just over there."

"How do you know?"

"Because I nearly helped them with their digging about half hour ago."

Whilst I was telling this to Woody, the CO crawled over.

"Where the bloody hell have you been?" You are supposed to report to me."

"Couldn't find you sir. They told me you had gone back down."

"I've been waiting for the Company, why aren't they here?"

Here we go I thought and told him the whole story. He waited a long time in silence. I thought, he doesn't believe me he thinks I've been skiving.

"So how close are the Krauts then?"

I described how they were much higher up the hill than we were and pointed to the right,

"Very near the skyline on the brow of the hill sir."

More silence, I decided to press my knowledgeable luck further,

"We're in a daft position here sir."

That caught his attention quickly enough,

"That's none of your concern," and he crawled away in the darkness.

I looked at Woody, "Did he give you any fags then?"

"No, perhaps he don't smoke."

"Yes he does, he's a tight-fisted sod. Let's get digging."

We carried on digging our slit trench; it was a reasonable depth when the Sergeant came over,

"Have you been upsetting the CO Darlington?"

"I only told him what I saw, Sarg."

"Well why wasn't I told that you were skiving about out there?" The Sergeant was peeved.

"There wasn't time to tell anybody anything. He came over here and told me to get the rest of the Company up here."

"So where are they then?" The Sergeant was trying to get back at me for ignoring him.

"Ah, so he didn't tell you the whole story, did he Sarg?"

I then told him all the facts, about the pounding the Company had suffered and the problem I had in getting back.

"Christ Almighty, we're sitting ducks up here."

I said that the rest of the Company had had it worse than we did but he wasn't consoled. He was quite right about sitting ducks though. We all knew how German counter attacks went; they would come screaming down the hill and if there were enough of them, they would overrun us. We were only Platoon strength, about twelve slit trenches well spaced out on a wide expanse of hill; there was a Bren gun of course, which the Sergeant would put in the best position but it wasn't enough and we knew it. According to the Sergeant, his orders were to go forward about a mile and dig in, that's why we were in this mess: keep digging.

It was almost daybreak when a runner came up the hill to us. When he got within shouting distance, he told the Sergeant to bring his men down. We didn't need the Sarg to relay the order, we all heard it and we were off. Normally the Sergeant would have said something like, "Keep your heads down lads, crawl or creep and don't bunch up", but we were half way down the hill before he had time to say anything, passing the surprised runner who was still waiting for the Sergeant's reply. When we were safe and sound and out of breath, the Sergeant caught up and gave us the expected bollocking.

"You bloody fools, you could have drawn fire down, showing yourselves like that."

But we didn't and we're still here. Sometimes a gut reaction is better than trying to be clever but we knew the Sarg was right. He was ten years older than us and probably had two kids and a mortgage, he was bound to think differently.

In the early hours of the morning, our artillery guns laid a heavy barrage on the hill and I like to think that that blitzkrieg had something to do with my information but I'll never know for sure. During the barrage on our Company, our own Lieutenant Dudman, had been killed. The CO had said nothing about it to us because he was a very popular officer; it was a sad loss. Finally the battle of Gemmano was over; it was a very bloody affair though not much was made of it in the British Press, all the headlines were still about Europe.

Chapter 15

Rest in Peace

Planners of the Italian Campaign had never expected this state of affairs; all the men tied up in the middle eastern area could have been used in the Second Front in Europe: but there we were, still at it and no sign of a let up. So the next best thing was to press on and get to Germany from the south but as we were only half way up Italy, there was still a long way to go. When we were pulled out of the line for a few days' break, officers would come and give lectures on the general state of things. ABCA talks they were called, Army Bureau of Currant Affairs. Even with my poor education, I could tell it was all rubbish. Getting to Germany from the south meant crossing the Alps, a sort of Hannibal in reverse and what about Switzerland, nobody must upset them because all the rich people sent their money there in case the war went badly for them. No gentlemen, no Third Front is possible at the moment, just get on with what you're doing; Rimini on your right flank coming up next.

Around this time there was one place I remember, it was San Marino because it was neutral and we had to go round it. Don't drop any mortars in their direction we were told. Looking down on this hallowed ground from a mountain top, I wondered why it had this status. How had they managed to stay out of a war, when all round them was in chaos? I had my own bias ideas of course; why didn't the ABCA talks tell us how Switzerland, Sweden, The Vatican and San Marino could stay out of a war that involved half the world? I think it was the Church, money and people in high places doing deals; none of this concerned us of course we still had the rest of Italy to conquer.

We were off again towards Bologna; it looked like

we were going to walk all the way with resistance from every building in our path. I preferred these skirmishes in small groups rather than main attacks in Battalion strength; there were never any officers about and more chance to look for loot but you needed good mates. There was a lot of sniping going on and you had to be alert. Yesterday a German rushed out of a house with a Schmeisser machine gun and took us by surprise. One of our mates, Ray, was killed before we had time to react; the Ted ran into another house. Ray Evans was a good mate and so we were determined to get the Kraut; we threw hand grenades through every window, talk about over kill.

On the long terraced road I was dogging Woody's footsteps, we were on the move in full strength. The enemy must have moved back a long way for us to be stretched along the road in this fashion. The occasional shell winged over to remind us we were not on our holidays. Although we had been marching up hill, the field to the side was flat and when we turned off the road down to the field the bank to our front was almost vertical. It gave a safe feeling and we started to bunch up. The word came down to take a rest and we flopped down on the grass in small groups. For the sake of a minute we could have chosen better because three yards away there was a dead bullock and the stench was overpowering. The beast had started to rot and the other guys moved away. Woody and I stayed where we were, the grass was dry and we were comfortable, but it was no good, Woody sat up and said,
"I can't stand anymore of this, I'm going to move up wind."

He got up and walked past the decaying bull, the bank we felt so safe behind was overgrown with heavy foliage, some of it sticking out at right angles. That's what I heard first, the mortars crashing through the bushes. I was over on my face before the first explosion, it was a full salvo of bombs. The Germans must have guessed we would come this way, protected from artillery but not from mortars that come straight down out of the sky. A second and third salvo came down before there was a break. When I looked up it was mayhem, casualties everywhere, anyone on their feet would have been hit.

I ran past the bull carcass to search for Woody: when I found him I was shocked at the state he was in, but he was alive. His mouth and jaw were stove in, he had a huge stomach wound and both his feet were off; but he was alive. Infantry soldiers were only obliged to carry a field dressing in the regulation uniform pocket but in action we used to pack shell dressings under the camouflage net on our helmet. I ripped the shell dressing from my head and unwrapped it but I didn't know what to do with it, where do you put such an inadequate item on wounds as severe as these. I laid it across his mouth but he pulled it away and started to mumble something. I leaned across his battered face and tried to understand but it was no good. He grabbed my arm with quite a strong grip but I could make no sense out of the sounds coming from his lacerated face. In desperation I looked round for help but it was carnage everywhere, no medics or stretchers.

I shouted, "Stretcher bearers, stretcher bearers."
The cry was taken up by squaddies trying to do something for the wounded.
"The medics are well to the rear, there'll be something on the main road," someone said.

That's it, I thought, do something positive, it's the only way to help Woody. Without waiting for more information I was off, jumping over bodies and heading back the way we had come. Once on the main road I ran with all speed and then the shells started coming over. I was surprised that this road had not been targeted when the battalion was here, the Krauts must have a good observation post nearby, they certainly knew where to put those mortars down on us. The shelling got heavy with several direct hits in the centre of the road. Up ahead I could see a burned out tank, I remembered passing it on the way up and I made for it like a cat on fire. It was a German Tiger tank and I dived under it, then I wished I hadn't. The explosions were rocking the vehicle and I thought the nearside track would go down in the ditch and with so little headroom I could be crushed.

At this late stage of the war, I had seen a lot of dead men and some were very good mates but this was all for Woody and I was wasting time not knowing what I was doing. He would have known if the position had been reversed, so ignoring the danger I got onto the road again and started running. I had no real idea of what I was looking for. It must have been another mile before I saw the Jeep with a Red Cross on it; I stopped to catch my breath. The white and red paint was all the encouragement I needed; now I could do something useful. Looking round I saw a ruined building with some activity going on, I dashed over and surprised the people inside.
"Quick, stretcher bearers come with me."
"We don't take orders from you mate."

I was wild, frantic and dangerous and in no mood for any arguments. I stuck my rifle viciously into the belly of the guy who spoke, he gasped and fled from the room shouting, "Sir, sir." The MO appeared and I turned my rifle on him. There was panic on his face as he tried to say.
"What's ...going...on in...here?" He could hardly get the words out. I gabbled at the officer, I don't even know if I was coherent but he got the drift and defused the situation by saying to the room,
"Four of you go with him."

I didn't stop to see who he was talking to, I was out of the door and waiting. They were taking too long. I went back in again, they were untying a bundle of stretchers.

"For fuck sake hurry up."

I know now that I was making matters worse but I wasn't thinking straight otherwise when we got outside I would have saved time by using the Jeep instead of running back up the road with four squaddies behind me trying to keep up.

We arrived back at the killing field, breathless. There was a lot going on and stretcher bearers were already at work. Someone much calmer than me had sorted it. I left the confused medics who had faithfully followed me; there was plenty of work for them anyway. I ran to the spot where I had left Woody, he was gone. I spoke to the nearest medic.

"He's already been taken, I tucked him up myself."

I persisted and described the wounds,

"Yes that's him."

"But he was alive wasn't he?"

"Oh yes, we're not collecting dead un's yet."

As I turned away he called me back, "His one foot wasn't gone, it was still in the boot tied to his ankle by the laces. I put the boot on the stretcher with the foot still in it. I don't know if it will make any difference, but you never know."

My mind mused on orthopaedics and the possibility of sewing feet back on but I asked one last question,

"Are you sure he was still alive?"

The medic had a lot of work to do but he took his time and made the answer quite clear, "Yes," he said.

Although I had a beef about medical orderlies, I had great faith in the hospitals. He was going to be all right, I was feeling less guilty now and thought about some of the good times we had had together. In Algiers, Egypt, Naples, Rome and a drunken binge in a wine cellar where we were so cold we shared a blanket by laying it on the floor and rolling over and over each other. We finished up wrapped in a cocoon with me on top and my face pressed against his.

"Woody," I said, "I'm going to be sick."

In a panic, he tried to get out of the way but the blanket was too tight. I was sick all over his face. We unrolled ourselves out of the blanket and staggered about the cellar floor laughing. You can't get a better mate than that; things were not going to be the same from now on...

As I walked between other wounded men I saw a tourniquet being applied to a man's arm and I was filled with guilt; was that what Woody was trying to tell me, "tourniquet, tourniquet"? I mumbled it to myself several times, getting more convinced with each time. If that was so, I had wasted valuable time with those stretcher men? Questions were crowding into my head. Could a severely injured man still have presence of mind to give instructions like that? I paid closer attention to the medic as he dealt with the severed hand, realising that I wouldn't have known how to apply a tourniquet anyway but that was no excuse and the guilt wouldn't go away.

"Darlington, get over here," the Sergeant's shout bought me back to reality.

"Get a move on and catch up with the others."

The Sergeant was rounding up dazed men. I wandered off, keeping my eye on the sky. Tranquillity had returned to this tragic place. All my schoolboy romantic notions about being in a war had long disappeared, probably about twelve months ago, five minutes after the first shot being fired. I had kept going because there were good times and they balanced out the times when I was scared to death. This was largely due to my mates, who were no doubt following the same kind of confused thinking but I was losing them fast. Woody's departure affected me more

164

than I cared to admit.

There were changes in the attitude of the men, especially those who had been with us since the landings. Several of us witnessed a sickening incident one morning as we walked through a defeated enemy position. A wounded German was sitting with his back to a tree, he was holding up his hand trying to get some assistance. One of the men walked over to him and kicked him full in the face, it must have killed him instantly. Unconcerned, the man joined the column with blood all over his boot. What makes a man behave like that and why didn't anyone say anything? A year ago, we would all have been horrified but real war is not sanitised like it appears in news clips on our television screens in the security of our own homes; it is brutal, dangerous and harrowing.

We had been pulled out of action to a reserve position behind the lines, it was quiet apart from the odd shell that landed near by. It was amazing, that kind of danger was of no consequence to those of us who had faced Nebelwerfers and German counter attacks, only the new boys worried.

It started as a normal day or as normal as this strife ridden conflict allowed. The trick on these occasions was to be invisible before some officer thought of something to improve his leadership skills. Cleaning ourselves and our equipment took all our time and we thought that we were safe but the CO had other ideas; day and night patrols. Patrols would range between terrifying and a down right skive, depending on what they were for. If it was intelligence gathering, it might have involved grabbing a prisoner, which meant getting very close to an enemy position. In 1943 we caught a Kraut Sergeant who was lost, but luck like that was very rare. If it was a reconnaissance patrol, it depended on who was leading it. It could be a medal hunting Lieutenant who could give you a hard time or

an NCO thinking, "We're not looking for trouble lads
are we?" So when the Sergeant came round with his
list we were apprehensive.

"It's just a walk along the river lads, nothing nasty."
"What river is that Sarg?" I asked.
"Does it matter?" he replied. He needed six men and
I was picked.
"Get a Tommy gun and be ready at 14.00 hours."
To get a Tommy you had to borrow one from a Corporal
so I looked round for a victim. I saw a tall guy whom I
knew back in Colchester, I had run against him in the
mile and I reminded him about it.
"Oh yes I remember, why didn't you stay there?"
"I'm a mental case, I like going on patrols, that's why I
need your gun," I made some idiot gestures.
"Oh no you don't, I've just cleaned it, sod off and try
somebody else."
"Don't be silly Corp; I've only got to call him over," and
I pointed to one of the officers. "Look, I promise I won't
fire it. That's fair isn't it?" and I meant it; all part of
my keep your head down policy. He had no choice
and we exchanged weapons. I asked him to look after
my famous Kukri to make him feel better.

I had no illusions about my role in the Army, I was
cannon fodder and I had chosen it. I could have sat
out the war in safety as a PT instructor at a training
camp in England but there was no job satisfaction for
my immature expectations. We could be thankful that
commanders of World War II were not as wasteful as the
1914-18 lot. Those Generals should have been tried
as War Criminals; things had changed for the better,
but drawing the enemy fire was still a legitimate army
tactic and I think that that is what we were about to
be used for. It is easy to work things out in retrospect
but none of these thoughts occupied our young minds
as we gathered round the Sergeant for a briefing.

"We've got a few miles to go before we get to the river,

but we're getting a lift back by Bren gun carrier, so we can get a move on and have a nice rest lads."

"What river is it Sarg?" I asked again.

"The River Po, not that it should matter to you," he replied.

The River Po, I thought. What a stupid name for a river, does it empty into a giant piss pot or something? I decided to have one more go,

"Why can't we go by carrier in the first place?"

"Because it wouldn't be a foot patrol then, would it?"

Of course, I had to give way to my Sergeant's superior knowledge. We all set off in single file, armed with automatic weapons; the weather was good the visibility was clear and the tourist brochures now remind me that this is a beautiful part of Italy. Some hours later, we arrived at the river. In calmer times I discovered it was not the Po anyway. It could have been any number of rivers running north like the Enza, the Taro or the Panaro, they all run into the Po Valley but we could not have made the main river in the time. Not that it would have made any difference to our Sergeant's geographic knowledge even if we had known that.

"Spread out along the river Po lads."

This far north we were well into the enemy's back yard; it took another four months for the American 5th and the British 8th Armies to cross the River Po in any strength and here we were flaunting ourselves. There were farm buildings near the bank and we walked between the buildings and the river. We were obviously being observed from the other side of the river and if this was a deliberate ploy to find out the Kraut gun positions and draw their fire, then it worked.

The 88mm shell hit the wall twenty feet in front of me and about three feet higher than my head. I was down with shrapnel in my body and my Tommy gun blown to pieces in my hands. There was no pain except for my little finger, left hand; all the fingers had been broken where they held the forward grip but only the little finger hurt. My right hand was total mess; the index finger was in the trigger guard and it hung down the back of my arm held on by bits of skin. I lay on my face and tried to explore the rest of my numb body. The only feeling I had was my left hand, so I used it to feel down my side. I could feel mangled flesh and the end of my tibia bone; I was convinced my legs had gone. My life had changed forever; no more Army and no more athletic aspirations.

They say that when you are about to die your whole life flashes before you, not so in my case, my mind was quite clear trying to imagine life without legs. The squaddie behind me was shouting; he had been hit the same time as me but I couldn't answer him, no words would form. I lay there silent, with visions of legless ex-Servicemen begging. I had seen a lot of that in my home town: were they begging for money or for their limbs to come back? I was jolted out of my stupor by mortars crashing down on the bank; one must have been a direct hit on my wounded colleague because I was covered in blood and gore. Survival instincts kicked in, I had to get below ground, into the river was the only option. With my left hand and broken fingers, I dragged myself the three yards to the edge of the bank and with one more effort I toppled over. I wasn't concerned with being in the water and drowning, only with getting off the bank. So far, they had only fired one shell but now all their concentration was on mortar fire and it rained down mercilessly.

It seemed like an age but eventually it stopped. I hadn't landed in the water, the bank wasn't straight down and I was on a ledge; faces appeared above me and looked down. I must have looked a hideous sight, apart from my own injuries some of the flesh from my colleague was still stuck to me. They lifted me out and carried me into the nearest building that offered some form of protection.

I still couldn't form any words but managed to mumble,

"My legs have gone."

"No, you're going to be all right mate."

They had to say that didn't they, how can you tell a legless man the truth; he might go mad? The Americans seemed to have a lot of medical equipment in the field to deal with situations like mine but the main thing was evacuation from the battlefield as soon as possible. Our chaps didn't carry any painkillers or drugs, only field dressings which are only bandages so there's a limit to what can be done but the lads did their best and I still could not feel any pain. A Bren gun carrier on reconnaissance was spotted and called over. The Sergeant ordered him to get me away quickly and the driver did just that. We went across fields, bumps and ditches, I was thrown into the air and desperately tried to protect my head, the rest of my body had no feeling. The driver wanted to get rid of his passenger; it was only luck that he came along when he did. I was interfering with more important work, it was such a relief when he stopped. I was transferred to a Jeep which had two stretchers laid across the back and one was already occupied.

No medical services were available, it was only a rendezvous point, so we set off quickly and because I was loaded on last I was over the wheels at the rear. A driver and two comrades side by side but at least we were on a road so the drive should not be too rough. By turning my head I could look at my companion; I could tell by his colour that he was not dead even though he appeared to be, he was so still with his eyes wide open staring at the sky. After a few miles shells started landing in the fields either side of us but we carried on until one hit the road. I shall never forgive the driver for what happened next; he stopped dead centre of the road, jumped out and ran for cover. I can't blame him for his panic action but he should have put his foot down and driven clear, instead we were left in an exposed position as more shells hit the road. The jeep was jumping about like a jack-in-a-box from the shelling. In that raised position we were likely to catch any shrapnel that was slicing and scything around so I had to get down. I had full movement in my neck and I rocked my head violently from side to side until I rolled right off the stretcher. Not being able to steady myself with my hands I crashed down into the road at the rear of the jeep; I could now add facial injures to the rest of my problems. With more neck and shoulder movements I was able to get my head under the vehicle. I couldn't see anything, blood from my nose was getting in my eyes. Finally the shelling stopped and the driver came out of hiding. I was lucky that he had seen my antics, if not he could have driven off straight over my head. Instead he picked me up and dropped me back on the stretcher, not thinking to check if the fresh blood on my face may have been caused by shrapnel. In all this time the lad next to me had not moved or even closed his eyes.

The next stop was a Forward Casualty Station where I received professional help and most importantly, blood. It was over four hours since I was hit and it was getting dark when they moved me into the medical tent. The tent was full and they were moving dead bodies out to make room. There was a lot of activity in this area so I could not say what happened to my silent buddy from the jeep. I was a lot calmer now that I had been treated and watching all the others around me took my mind off my condition. Bad as I was, this tent was full of people far worse. Only the seriously wounded were brought in here and a lot of dead bodies were moved out. This was a very sombre and silent place and you would expect a lot of painful cries instead of silence. I was in no pain, I expect my nervous system had closed down.

I was encased in plaster; my left hand wasn't too bad, but my right was huge like a giant club though strangest of all, my lower body was a great lump of plaster with no way of knowing what was in there.

"You've got to be able to travel well," I was told, the implication being that I was to be treated like a parcel.

"It doesn't matter about looking pretty, the thicker the plaster the better."

It all made sense, after all they were not treating road accidents with hospitals twenty minutes away. I lay in the tent thinking about all the wrong things, I needed to talk to a doctor. Orderlies saying, "You'll be all right," was not what I needed to hear. The doctors were too busy to chat and the Padre was only concerned with my soul, so I would have to wait and worry. The size of my mummified body was creating strange illusions that was I deformed? I had a restless and agitated night and some pain which would have been easy to cope with if it had not been accompanied by terrible itching which I could do nothing about. Don't despair Al, take another look around the tent; being with these men had a sobering affect on me.

There was something going on the next morning, another delivery of parcels to unknown destinations. I was back on a jeep again but strapped down this time and I didn't feel too well. It was only a short journey before we turned into a large field and there it was, a Dakota, the first aircraft I had ever seen close up. The DC3 Dakota was a workhorse used for every thing and one of very few aircraft which survived the war to be used in civilian life for years afterwards. They carried hundreds of troops and tons of supplies and the one I was looking at was about to transport broken men to the repair shop. It looked grand with its white fuselage and huge Red Cross.

It was near the end of 1944 and I was about to have

my first ride in an aeroplane: I remember being taken on board still on the stretcher. Inside there were racks either side so that the stretcher could be clipped on without handling the patient. The small gangway between enabled the medical staff to get up and down to deal with the drips that were suspended above every case. The plane was loaded from one end so when you were in position you could not see what was going on but you could hear the traffic as the jeeps came and the plane slowly filled up. Suddenly there was a roar and the Dakota shuddered, we were off. I clearly remember being loaded onto that plane but not being taken off; somewhere on that flight I lost consciousness. Whether it was induced or natural I don't know but when I came round, I was in hospital 350 miles behind the front line at a place called Bari. Safe from Tedeschi paratroops, safe from German shells, safe from anti-personnel bombs and safe from being shot at. Life was good, still alive if not kicking.

Myself (left) and Woody in a quiet moment between the bullets.
Woody died simply because his luck ran out

Chapter 16

How to salute without hands

When I was able to take in my hospital surroundings my first guess was Naples, but as I was in a side ward, I couldn't see very much. In fact, until I was informed by a nurse, I had never heard of Bari. I found out that it was opposite Naples on the other side of Italy. The nurse also told me I had arrived two days ago and had been in surgery already. The doctor wanted to talk to me about it.

"Good, I'm looking forward to that, go and get him."

"Don't give me orders young man; I hold a commission, Lieutenant to you."

"So we're in a military hospital are we? Like the 93rd in Naples, sir."

That made her smile and she warned me to watch out for Matron,

"She's a Major and a matriarch as well, so you'll soon be in the guano."

I could only assume that that was something nasty but she was a very nice nurse and with a final remark, "I'll tell the doctor; he's a Captain by the way," and a winning smile, she was off.

Left on my own I had a good look at myself, the plaster was still there, but different. There was a cradle over my legs and I could see two separate casts so they were still there, what a relief. The fingers on my left hand were visible in the plaster, stiff and straight but the right still looked like a club. I was finished off with sticking plaster over my eye and down the side of my nose.

I looked around the ward to see if anyone was in worse shape and some were. Most had cradles over and intravenous drips in place but they looked cheerful, not like that Forward Casualty Station. The reason was obvious; look what they had left behind.

In due course the doctor got around to me and his opening remark was,

"How you feeling son?"

The 'son' made me feel uneasy that this was going to be a sympathy chat.

"Well I'm glad to see my legs are still there, sir."

"Ah yes, that's what I want to talk to you about."

My unease shifted into a higher gear.

"The right leg is going to be all right, you're young and time will sort that out, but the left...a few years ago we would have had no chance of saving it..."

My gaze shifted to the left plaster and on second examination, it was a lot different from the right. I could no longer hear the doctor; my images were back, from a non-legged man to a one legged man. I had seen them, rows of medals and a crutch. How many medals are they going to give me?

"...but with Penicillin now available there's a good chance," the doctor kept going. It was the first time I had heard of Penicillin; it's taken for granted now. It was a British discovery before the war that was going nowhere until the Yanks took it up and started to produce it in quantity.

The doctor was very proud of the stuff,

"It's still very expensive, your body is worth a lot of money already, we can only use it where there is a danger of gangrene."

There's no doubt that many amputees owe their lives to this wonder drug. The doctor closed by saying,

"I promise you this, every time you come out of surgery I'll tell you the truth."

At eighteen years and five months, the truth can't hurt me can it?

The doctor's visit over, I took stock of my circumstances. Somewhere between getting wounded and now, Christmas had come and gone and I don't remember it happening. I remember last Christmas because we didn't have one, this time I wasn't even there. I knew

I was going to be hospitalised for a long time. Plan A, sit up and make the best of it. Sitting up wasn't that easy because the stitches in my stomach kept catching in my gown but propped up with pillows in a half up position and by keeping still, I was able to have a good look round.

There was a guy with a cradle on his back walking up and down the ward, everyone was calling him 'Tex'. He stood at the end of my bed with his legs in a bent stance. The curved cradle showing above his head forced him to lean forward, he looked like a giant banana. With his arms loosely at his side, he turned to me and made a grab for his invisible guns,
"Bang, bang, got yer. They call me Tex," he said.
"Now I can see why," I replied.
"I'll tell you my story before you ask why I look so ridiculous."
He was great fun and I listened carefully while he recounted his sad tale.

He was wounded while being taken prisoner and the Germans wanted to take him along with them. Some Krauts would have shot him rather than bother. The German commander was a gentleman and had his own reasons for being so helpful. They were doing all right until the British got too close and the wounded man was slowing down their escape. The German officer said they would have to leave him and agreed to make him comfortable by the side of the road.
"The British will find you in a few hours so you'll be all right."

As a final gesture of goodwill, the officer took off his Greatcoat and wrapped it around Tex, saluted him and was off; but the British didn't find him first, did they, some Italian civilians did. It may have been the German coat that triggered off their vicious attack but when it was obvious that he was British it made no difference. They stripped him naked and pulled him

176

all over the road and that's when his back got broken, then they left him for dead.

"A patrol found me and I finished here; what happened to you then?"

"Nothing glamorous like that," I said, "one shell came over and I was down."

"Oh, is that it then?"

He sounded disappointed so I thought I would cheer him up a bit.

"I've been done before, with the American 5th Army, they still owe me a medal."

"Why a medal?" he said.

"Because all their troops get the Purple Heart for wounds received in action," I replied.

This wasn't generally known by everybody then because Hollywood hadn't got round to telling them.

"Blimey, we only get a small bar on the sleeve and they get more money as well."

We both agreed that the Yanks got more of everything, Tex and I were going to get on fine. He introduced me to some of the other characters in the ward and that's when I had my first brush with the tank Sergeant.

I leaned away from Tex as he told me his story and looked across the ward. There was another patient also leaning out and looking past his leg cradle. We stared at each other for a moment then he said,

"Hallo baby face, what are boy soldiers doing in here? Where's your mommy then?"

"Bollocks to you too," I replied and turned back to Tex.

"What's his problem?" I asked.

"A mine got his tank. He lost both his feet, but he got out of the burning vehicle and ran several yards on the stumps before he collapsed."

The Sergeant was still going on but I didn't lean out so he couldn't see me.

"Too bad about his feet, but it didn't stop his big mouth did it!"

"Live and let live," said Tex.

I didn't let on my private thoughts that the Sergeant wouldn't have lived long outside this ward.

As the weeks went by, there were other bouts of excitement. One day they carried a Gurkha into the ward. When he was fit to talk he made a lot of friends, his English was good. On one occasion, quite unexpectedly, a group of British officers from the Indian Division turned up and stood round his bed. They were surprised he was in our ward, apparently he was an officer. When he was picked up on the battlefield nobody bothered to check. His clothing was in such a mess and with his dark skin it was a natural mistake and he was in no condition to say anything. He was Subadar, which is a Viceroy Commission with all the privileges of a British Captain. His brother officers wanted to move him out of our ward but he said, "No, I've made so many friends in here."

That wasn't the end of the Johnny Gurkha story. In due course, they brought in a German soldier straight from surgery and still unconscious. They put him in the next bed to our friend from Nepal. This often happened when the operating theatre was under pressure; he would go to the right ward later. When the German came round the first thing he saw was the grinning face of Johnny Gurkha and he screamed the place down. The Kraut had been taken prisoner by the Gurkhas, they had stood around him with their Kukris drawn and threatened to castrate him. Then a mortar shell had landed among them and that put paid to any other business. Can you imagine how the man felt, after all that, when he woke up and the first thing he saw was a Gurkha; it was more than the Ted could stand and they moved him out of the ward very quickly.

As soon as I came out of surgery the next time, the doctor returned with the news as he had promised. "You're going to keep your leg but it will be stiff, it's not possible to fix your knee."

My images were back; from a no leg man, to a one leg man, to a stiff leg man but at least the news was getting better all the time. I tried to think of some stiff legged characters; Long John Silver, no that was no good, he had a wooden leg, the cowboy Hop-along Cassidy, I didn't know if his leg was genuine or not but that's what they would call me, Hop-along Al; the doctor was still talking,

"We'll cut your injections from every three hours to every four and we'll start some skin grafting on the right leg."

"What about this?" I held up the club on my right hand.

"We've done the best we can with that, you'll have to wait and see."

As an afterthought he added, "I have put your finger back on."

Because of my hands, I couldn't feed myself and this gave the Sergeant more ammunition.

"Mommy's going to feed you, why don't you have a bottle?"

His insults were beginning to depress me and reference to a bottle brought on more innuendo because I had to call for assistance for even the basic functions. When assistance came, I was always glad if it was a nurse. They were more professional than the Royal Army Medical Corp (RAMC) orderlies who would exchange nods and winks with the Sergeant adding to his fun. I was in some pain as the wounds started to heal and my four hourly injections went on over twenty four hours a day. During the night, a nurse would inject without wakening me but an orderly would crash his tray and syringe down on the locker and say it was the rules. I had to be woken up in case I rolled over and broke the needle. Maybe it was the laissez-faire policies of the hospital that let these men do as they liked. When the skin grafting began, the surgeon would mark out the donor areas on my backside where the skin would be

179

taken from. An orderly would scrub the skin until it was raw, a nurse would wipe the skin with antiseptic and cotton wool, tape gauze over it and that was that, no violent scrubbing needed. Skin grafting was painful enough without extra agro.

Hospital life was boring for most of the time but there were people behind the scenes trying to make it more bearable. A group of young Italians with guitars came round and entertained us. Their popular number in English was Paper Doll, it's strange that I should still remember most of the words. My favourite was Momma sung by an Italian tenor, this was great stuff and probably the reason why I became an opera buff. Self-pity, pain and shock were all good reasons why I hadn't thought about Woody. When I did, I asked for the Padre to come and see me. Padres were busy in places like that and it took a few days. The Padre was a Captain and a very nice bloke: they always were. Just think of the difficulties, being part of a killing machine and at the same time preaching peace and goodwill to all men.

I told him about Woody and the possibility that he could be in the hospital somewhere.
"That will be easy to check," he said.
I think he was glad that my request was practical and not on a higher plane. I suggested he checked the Naples hospital as well.
"He may have been sent home," he replied hopefully.
"I doubt that sir, he was in a worst shape than me and they've made it very clear that nobody goes home until they are fit to travel by sea."
"What about writing to him then?"
I held up both arms, "Sorry, I'll go and do some checking," and he was off.
After he left, I thought he could have written a letter for me but no matter, I'll get a nice nurse to do it when he's checked all the other possibilities. The possibility that Woody could finish up in the next bed raised my

hopes tremendously. I leaned outwards and looked across at the Sergeant; yes you bastard the two of us would soon sort you out.

I came out of another session of surgery and whilst I was under the anaesthetic, they had removed the plaster from my left hand. I still had splints on two of the fingers but I could use it quite well. Now I could use a spoon and feed myself. This small improvement made a big difference to my self-esteem. With my new dexterity, I decided to check my locker to see what I had left of my loot; to my amazement there was nothing. I knew what had happened and I was determined to make a fuss about it. I called a nurse and asked about my personal effects.
"Everything you had on you when you came in, is in the locker."
"I can't find anything."
This gave the Sergeant a chance to butt in,
"Has he lost his teddy bear?"
The nurse told him to keep quiet and moved the locker away from the bed.
"Have you looked in the bottom of the cabinet?"
"No, I can't get down there."
My movement was still restricted by the plaster on my legs.
"Let's have a look before everyone gets excited."
The nurse was quite right, she could see that I was angry and maybe she had seen this problem before. The nurse was calling from below the bed level.
"There's your pay book here."
"Bugger the pay book, where are the watches?"
"Are you sure you had a watch?"
I had to be careful here, there had been one on one wrist and two on the other.
"Yes, it was a birthday present."
"Well, there's no watch here."
"What about rings?"
"No jewellery either." The nurse was getting concerned,
"Was it valuable?" she said.

Was it, I wondered? I never had the chance to find out and it wasn't an 'it', there were four of them.
"No," I replied. I didn't bother to mention a large brooch.
"There's a wallet with some papers and a medal."
She brought the items round the bed for me.
"There should be some bullets there as well."
"There's no way they would allow those in here."
I explained about the broken bullets I was going to make into a necklace.
"There's nothing like that in here."

So that was that, thanks RAMC. They wouldn't have understood the significance of the bullets but what made them leave my German souvenirs, conscience perhaps? It must have happened at the Causality Clearing Station, there was plenty of opportunity. Some would say, easy come easy go but I would not agree that it was easy come.

The weeks rolled by and although my medical condition improved, my mental state didn't. I was about to enter the worse period of my eighteen years; the nightmares started. A lot of the men had them, there was nothing unusual about that. Mine were about the near tragedies that had happened the previous year. All had been lucky escapes, like the burst of machine gun fire that went through the corner of my leather jerkin and the time that I was on observation with an Artillery Officer and an armour piercing shell went though two walls of the cottage we were in. I was standing in the corner of the room and the shell was only ten inches away. Memories of my shattered helmet and Woody treading on that land mine were all thoughts which raced through my mind. By all the law of averages, I should be dead. What was I worrying about; here I was in a nice clean bed, I had made it so why should I be so jumpy?

I don't remember what the final thing was that pushed

me over the edge, it may have been another jibe from the Sergeant or another chorus of Paper Doll from the Italian musicians. I just lay back on the pillows starring into space which became centred on the bottle hanging from the stand by my bed. I'd had intravenous drip bottles round me since I was first hit and never taken much notice of them but this time my eyes were on the glass phial and the little tap that controlled the drip of clear liquid past the small section of glass tube. My eyes followed it down unseen in the brown rubber tube to the back of my hand and now that there was no plaster on the hand, it was the latest position for the intravenous. I'd had transfusions into my arms and the veins showed puncture marks in many places but the left hand was the most convenient and I stared at it like I had never seen it before. If kept still I could just feel the featherlike touch as the liquid entered the vein, then my attention went back to the glass tap to wait for the next time.

I stared at the drip and then counted the milliseconds and then the slight flutter as it reached my hand, nothing to it. This was now a full-time occupation, my mind had something to concentrate on. What I didn't realise was that when the liquid reached its destination, I had started to twitch. Like most schoolchildren, I liked to read horror stories and one I remember was the Chinese water torture. The victim was strapped down and a drip of water splashed onto his forehead every few seconds, the story would explain how the unfortunate victim would go stark raving mad in a few hours. A bit far fetched and we didn't really believe it, did we? My experience was about to prove otherwise. The twitch became a jerk and the jerk became a spasm. I tried to look-away but I was mesmerized. My eyes always went back to the bottle and now my timing was perfect. I was ready a split second before the explosion and cried out, my shouting soon attracted the attention of a nurse. "Well don't look at the bloody thing then."

The nurse showed her irritation by pushing the bottle stand noisily to the rear of the bed. It was obvious that bullying tactics were not the answer to what is now known as Post Traumatic Stress Syndrome. By turning my head, I could still see it. I knew the liquid was coming for me; there was no escape. Explosions, one after the other, more screaming. I don't know how long this crazy period lasted but I was told later by medical staff and patients that it caused quite a commotion. I was shouting about dead bodies that wouldn't get up and help me and detached parts of my own body that kept talking while they joined up again.

What I'll never understand is why I was such a problem. We had been at war for over four years and there was the experience of the First World War with its thousands of shell shocked victims. There must have been hundreds of people like me and yet there was so little understanding. Post Traumatic Stress is now studied and treatment given for minor tragedy, counselling taken to the point where it has become a joke but back in the forties it was, "Pull yourself together man", or if you were lucky a short rest because of battle fatigue.

When I became 'normal' again, the ward had moved on and there were several new faces. The Sergeant had gone, I was glad to see, but so had Tex and I missed him. The upside was that most of the chaps hadn't seen me go 'nuts' so I didn't have to talk about it. I still felt embarrassed by my breakdown, my immature thinking was still in the macho mould.

Better news came when the nurse told me that the doctor had said she could remove the plaster from my right hand anytime. It was a big job and she wanted uninterrupted time to deal with it. I waited with great expectations for the hour to arrive. Ever since the doctor had told me that he had sown my finger back on, I had looked at this huge lump of plaster with some amusement. It looked like a giant club with no inkling of what was inside, so when the nurse turned up with a saw, the whole ward was interested. I must say I had no pain from this injury, apart from an itching inside the plaster and the weight on the end of my arm. I anticipated that all must be well so when the nurse started sawing it was jokes all round the ward. She weakened it with saw cuts and started to break it away; finally the hand came free. All the fingers were spread out and stiff with no movement at all; that was to be expected but when I turned the hand over and looked at the palms, Frankenstein came to mind. The stitching had been removed but all the stitch marks were there, ugly and red with wheals of raw flesh bulging between them as if someone had sown up an over stuffed pillow case. It looked like it had been repaired by a six year old.

"I can't believe this," I gasped.

The nurse turned on the charm.

"With therapy you'll soon have some feeling in the fingers."

I felt round the tips, there was some feeling in some of them but the worst was my index finger.

"That's been sown on out of line and it's dead."

The digit was twisted to the right and bulged with welts like a mountain range. I could not believe what I was looking at and made uncomplimentary remarks about doctors. This upset the nurse and she said that she would report me. As she stormed off I shouted at the top of my voice,

"If this is what my fucking hand is like, are you sure my leg is on the right way round?"

There was no need for the nurse to report me, there was a doctor in the ward and he had heard every word. He came storming up to my bed. He was no longer Mr Nice Guy but an Army Captain, come to sort out insubordination in the ranks.

"What do you think you're playing at, upsetting people

185

who are trying to do their best?"

He was right of course but considering the state of my hand, I thought I had some leeway though he wasn't having any.

"There are people in here that are worse off than you."

Right again but that's always the case; he calmed down and went on.

"Considering the facts, your leg is doing remarkably well. The remarks you made are totally out of order."

It's easy to forget that this was a Military Hospital and all the doctors and nurses were officers, so it was a good idea to put on a show every now and again to remind the plebs how they stood and this officer was going to make the most of my indiscretions. While he ranted on, I was thinking of stuff I had read about discipline in Victorian Military Hospitals. There were regulations about how a limbless man should lie to attention when Matron made her rounds. I almost burst out laughing when I thought of my hand saluting with all the fingers stuck out, the officer would think I was taking the piss.

"Are you paying attention to what I said Darlington?"

"Yes sir, but it wasn't the leg sir, it was this."

I held up my hand and it momentarily put him off his stride. He had to rethink, he squeezed my fingers together and let them go, they shot back again. He did this several times, I was like a bookie trying to get 5 to 1 on the race course.

"You'll be having physiotherapy soon and that will help."

"But look at this sir," and I pulled at the finger to make it look worse.

"You are lucky to have a hand anyway, the opinion was to take it off, putting your finger on was a gamble."

"But it's not on straight, sir."

"For God's sake wait till you have therapy and no more smart ass remarks."

After he had left, I decided to apologise to the nurse

but all she said was, "foul mouth" and then ignored me.

In any group of men there are always some trouble-makers and I had no wish to be regarded as one of them. My treatment since leaving the battlefield had been excellent, I had no real complaints but my hand had been a shock. As for the rest of me; my left hand apart from a crooked little finger looked normal. The skin grafts on my right leg were healing well in spite of the rough treatment by the orderlies. The only mystery was my left leg; it was still a case of wait and see. Having not seen it without plaster, I had no idea what to expect and only the itching inside the plaster reminded me that there was anything there. What I should have been worrying about was whether I would be employable after the war but I was young with no dependants and it didn't seem to matter.

As we moved further into 1945, it didn't seem to us that the end was nigh, even though the war ended in May that year. According to our newspaper, the Stars and Stripes, the Americans were in trouble on the river Reno, perhaps they missed us after all. The Canadians were doing much better but so they should, they were big lads. Sorry, I'm not being fair; it's easy to be smug when you're tucked up in a clean warm bed. Rumours and speculation were all we had got to think about when all the cutting and stitching was done and the trips to the operating theatre were less frequent. The more politically genned up types in the ward were talking about a socialist state, where nobody would have to work anyway; so that was all right then. That stuff was all over my head so I just kept lusting after the nurses instead.

You could always tell when there was going to be a transfer of patients from the hospital; the musicians gave us an extra chorus of Paper Doll before they brought the hat round and the nuns were doing a roaring trade in crucifixes and rosary beads. Some of us were being transferred to Naples, the last stop before the hospital ship. We got on to the nurses to find out who was on the list but we were always the last to know. This time I was on the list and looking forward to visiting the 93rd General for the second time and I told all the lads that they had nothing to worry about.

"I've been there before, when I bought it the first time a year ago, it's a smashing place."

There's always a sceptic and he's usually the tall thin bloke with glasses.

"What if we're strafed while we're still in the ambulance convoy?"

That was a horrid thought, to get done just as you are about to go home.

"Good God man, the Ted's haven't been able to put anything in the air for months, we're winning for fuck sake, don't you listen to the news?"

We waited for the official version about how they were going to move us.

We bumped our way across Italy from the Adriatic to the Mediterranean. All the other lads in the ambulance were from the 8th Army, so I was able to expand on the delights of being in the 5th Army. As we were approaching my original killing fields, I gave them the full treatment.

"Yes, we did all this side from Salerno to Rome; I saw Vesuvius go up in '44."

This proved to be an interesting talking point. I was a product of the 1930s when using your imagination was never encouraged, so I was completely self-taught. I think they got the impression that I was running down the mountain chased by boiling lava.

"We got covered in black soot." That part was true anyway.

I told them about the red light area down by the docks and how much they could expect to pay. I always surprised the older soldiers with my know-how but I had been in Italy for a life time.

"You'll be able to see Vesuvius if it's still smoking, when we get near to the city."

No, they weren't interested; they wanted to hear more about the prostitutes. Ok here goes; I started to pronounce the city in Italian, Napoli sounds much more sexy although I couldn't see what difference it made, these lads wouldn't be visiting any fleshpots however it was pronounced.

"I'm not up to date with inflation but I imagine the cigarette has given way to the mighty dollar now that law and order as returned."

I had to explain this in more detail to one of them. What never ceased to amaze me was how naive some of the older lads were: they were a product of the 1920s, too young for the 1914-18 war and too old to learn anything from this one.

The last leg of the journey was through the metropolitan city. In the windowless ambulance, we could only hear what was going on but it sounded normal with little to remind us of a military presence. We came to a stop in the hospital grounds, the doors crashed open and orderlies lifted us out and put us on to trolleys.

When I had arrived here before, flat on my back, I hadn't paid much attention to my surroundings. This time, sitting up on the trolley, I could see a long tunnel from the ambulance bay leading into the interior and the snake of trolleys as they made their way down the long corridor. We were met by medical and welfare staff in the business part of the hospital and a doctor asked me how I was feeling.

"Take the plaster off and I'll walk out of here, sir."

Proving you were fit to travel seemed to be the name of the game.

"You're not going to be walking anywhere for a long time son," was his glum reply.

We went off to our various wards, settled in and met our new companions. The situation was the same as the last hospital but now there was this great expectation; we were going home, a group of men all in the same boat waiting for the same boat.

I had some feeling in my left foot which was very encouraging and by pushing down I could feel my ankle getting stronger. I kept this exercise up until finally I cracked the plaster. Then I discovered that I could not lift my foot up again: this was a condition that I was going to have live with for a long time. The doctor was pleased and said the plaster was due to come off anyway but I would be home in a matter of weeks so it was best left until then. The nurse reinforced my ankle and wrapped more plaster round my thighs. I couldn't sit up but I was nicely packaged and made ready for the boat.

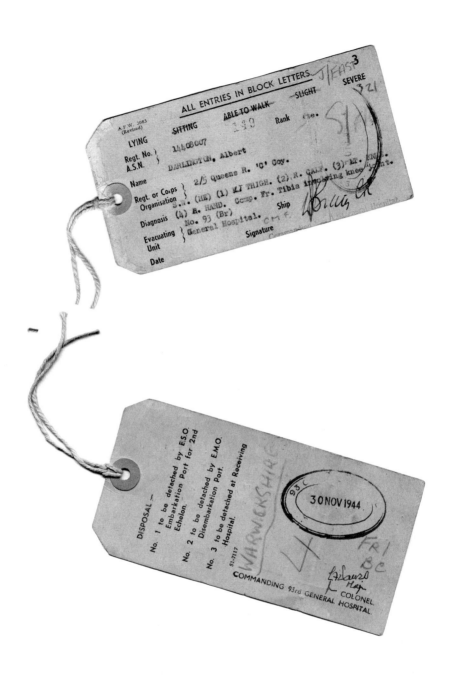

*The last of three labels which were tied to me for my journey home,
showing who I was, my Regiment, what my injuries were and what
stage of the journey I was on*

The hospital ship was called the Orangie; it may have been Dutch. It was a grand sight even from my horizontal position. Stretcher bearers carried us on board: we had coloured tickets tied to us which decided which part of the ship we went to and disability was the deciding factor not rank. I was put in a cabin with a double bunk, there was no choice, I went on the bottom one. There was a porthole but I couldn't see out of it, it didn't matter though as this was a luxury so different from when I had come out here in '43. I lay there on my bunk listening to the hustle and bustle as the cabins on either side filled up, wondering whom my cellmate would be. Presently a nurse came into the cabin, very brisk and businesslike and followed by two bearers with a stretcher at shoulder height; they deposited the body on the top bunk and left. I immediately tried to start a conversation with my roommate.

"Its no good," said the nurse, "he can't reply."
"Can he hear me?" I asked.
"Yes, he's Canadian and very ill, I shall tend to him for the whole voyage."
"Do I get a personal nurse as well?"
"I shall see to you as well, you cheeky sod." It was obvious we were going to get on fine.

Food is always good on a boat, the bread is baked daily and the orderly said that I could have as much as I liked
"Can you feed yourself?" he asked.
"Yes, but I can't sit up."
My hands were clumsy but I could manage on my side so he fixed me up with a low table, level with the bunk.
"What about him up top?" I enquired.
"He's on liquids, the nurse sees to him."
I tried talking to my cabin-mate but apart from a bit of shuffling, he made no other signs.

Sometime during the night when every one was asleep, we sailed.

Look around the mountains, in the mud and rain,
See the scattered crosses, some which have no name,
Heartbreak and toil and suffering gone,
The lads beneath them slumber on,
They are the D-Day Dodgers who'll stay in Italy.

Chapter 17

"It's a loony bin mate"

We must have been mid Mediterranean the very next day when God smiled on me and gave me a bonus for all the good things I must have done in my life. I very nearly became religious. It all started when the lights came on and the ship began its day. The nurse came in and carried out her chores, she fiddled with my bunk and pillows and we chatted. As a full Lieutenant in the Queen Alexandra's Imperial Military Nursing Service, she could have been toffee nosed and frosty but she joked with me and we kept our voices down in respect for the poor bugger up top. It was difficult for her to make up the bed on the upper bunk and the Canadian couldn't help so she said to me,
"I shall have to come round to the end of the bunk to get at his pillows."
She looked down at me and said,
"You'll have to move your head."
I looked up at this gorgeous female and said, "I can't sit up."
I had used this statement many times before but never had it had such significance,
"Then you'll have to keep your head still and close your eyes."
With that she put one foot on the wooden bunk at the side of my head, grabbed the top rail and swung herself up, then she planted her other foot on the opposite side of my face.
"Have you got your eyes closed"?
"Yes," I lied.
"Keep them that way, I shall not be long."

Can you imagine the run of luck I was having? I was wounded badly enough to have a cabin and not to be one of the walking wounded down below; by pure chance I'd been put on the lower bunk; I'd got a

British nurse and not an American one because they all wore slacks; she was a darling and not a dragon and bless the nurse that wrapped me up so tightly in plaster that I couldn't sit up. With luck like that there was no chance that we would get torpedoed on the way home.

"Take as long as you like it's no problem." I made the remark hopefully, but she was on to me,

"You're a cheeky sod."

This was the morning ritual and we were at sea for a week. I tried to tell my Canadian mate but he just rolled about, so I don't know if it excited him or just annoyed him. With all the food and the nurse's knickers, I was sorry when we sailed into Southampton. There was a band playing and it was awful, it was pouring with rain and this made the poor band sound even worse. The stretcher bearers were grumpy because they were soaking wet. As they picked me up first I was able to see the face of my colonial friend, his expression told me nothing. Perhaps I was being unfair, nobody could do anything about the weather but it was not only that, the whole thing was so third rate. We had all seen films about what happened when the Yanks went Stateside and whilst we didn't expect that kind of glamour, this was a very poor show. I have never in my life considered myself privileged and certainly not in the 'Noblesse Oblige' sort of way but I was a child of the British Empire and had come to accept that we must be better than everyone else. This may account for the fact that for the first time I felt ashamed to be British; it was such a poor show that greeted us when we docked.

With ground sheets over us to keep out the worst of the weather, we were bundled into the ambulances that were lined up on the quay. There were no news cameras about as far as I could tell; happy smiling victorious soldiers is what they wanted, not a boat load of broken men. It was a very short journey to the next stage, the railway station. I have already said that railway stations in wartime have a certain romance but not this one, it was grim. The carriages had been adapted to slot in stretchers and we were packed in to the roof. These guys could have given lessons to the old slave ship owners.

I remember one unpleasant incident just after we started to move. An orderly had just passed me carrying a bucket of water when someone cried out for a drink; the orderly replied that he was too busy. I think I was the first to mouth off some obscenity. "You miserable bastard, give the man a drink." He came back down the carriage, I thought he was going to hit me with the bucket but there were several people barracking him now and he had second thoughts. He stood by me and said, "I'm on my own, I've got a lot on." He got no sympathy from me, I was still angry about all the loot that was stolen by the RAMC orderlies. Our version of RAMC was - Rob All My Comrades.

We rumbled to a stop somewhere and were transferred to ambulances again. From my prone position, I couldn't tell what the hell was going on, I just had to be patient. Not only could I not see anything but when they slid me out of the vehicle, my vision was still limited. What I could see was that the place we were parked outside was big and the weather was still awful, which didn't enhance the drab looking building facing me. Whilst I didn't expect any hospital to be the same as the Italian ones that I had spent the last few months in, I thought that perhaps it would be better inside. One of the stretcher bearers put me right, "It used to be a loony bin, mate."

An answer like that was bound to get me to make further enquires. Apparently it was a mental institution which had been taken over by the military, such was the demand for hospital beds in the fifth year of war and all the inmates had been moved to prefabricated buildings in the grounds. We could see them from the upper windows on the other side of a wall. They would crowd together and march round a flower bed, suddenly stop and shout at the sky, then about turn. It was very strange the first time I witnessed it. I don't know if any of them were war casualties, if so they were worse off than we were.

The wards were big, thirty to forty beds; they didn't have entertainment in the ward but there was a theatre in the hospital and a show every month. The food didn't compare with the hospital ship but you can't have everything.

A lot of things happened to me in this place and I shall relate them in the order I remember them. The first thing of note was the removal of my plaster. A young nurse cut it away and I think she was as excited as I was to see what it would reveal - it was a mess. My right leg was looking good, all the skin grafts had healed and apart from the calf having no feeling, it was fine. The dead part had a certain entertainment value, I could stick pins in it and that became my party piece. The left leg though was a different situation. The nurse and I stared at it without comment. No amount of skin grafts would ever make it look pretty. So much of the muscle had been torn away that all the skin had sunk. The kneecap didn't look too bad but there was no movement in it. My foot was hanging down but I could press down against the nurse's hand, however I could not then bring the foot back up again. She called the doctor to see and the movement impressed him.
"It's better than I expected." I couldn't agree.
"Over the years some of this muscle loss will fill out and it won't look so bad."
The doctor was putting on a good show.
"I'll put you on an intensive physiotherapy program."
The physiotherapy team were all young girls, in fact

the hospital was staffed with young girls and people brought out of retirement. The war had creamed off all the males and there were some memorable occasions with the ex-retired staff. One was the ward sister who was a cow but more about her later. Another was a nerve specialist who came up from London every Saturday. Remember all these people were from the old school, trained in the 1920s and 30s when discipline was harsh. Another guy would connect me up to a machine and work my foot with electricity, it was called Faraday treatment. I don't think it's in use anymore and the sun bed method certainly isn't. Long before sun beds were invented, they used to sit you round a carbon stick, an electrode was placed near and an arc of sparks would jump the gap, like modern electric welding. We just sat there, wearing dark glasses, not knowing if it was doing us any good but it was a daily treatment.

In place of the plaster I wore a Thomas splint, a two inch strip of sticky tape went down each side of the leg, leaving a loop at the foot with a piece of wood in it. An iron frame went over and fastened at the thigh, with tension on the wood my leg could be pulled straight. This was the most important treatment and three times a day the girls from the physio department removed the splint and worked on my knee, getting a degree of movement was a major success. They gave me exercises for my hands, which included making soft toys. Cutting out the felt and stitching was easy enough but I didn't always stick to the script and this got me into trouble one Saturday morning. Around a dozen junior doctors were waiting for the famous nerve specialist; he was a very grumpy old man and didn't seem to be able to cope with young girls; I on the other hand could.

I had been making them laugh with some of my toy alterations and sitting on my locker were two toy animals that I was proud of. They all stood round my bed while the great man pointed at my foot and lectured on about sciatic nerves. One of the girls spotted my cross-eyed elephant and nudged her mate, she looked round and saw the daft looking donkey and started to giggle, others joined in. The consultant turned round to see what was causing the distraction. Not impressed with my artistic bent he swiped the two toys off the locker right across the ward, then gave the students a bollocking for not paying attention. He never said a word to me, it was beneath him to talk to a patient.

Two weeks later, there was another kafuffle with the same consultant. His usual drill was to have one of the students act as spokesman for the group and they would come and see me, to familiarize themselves with the case. This girl was new and late, she rushed up to me after the consultant had entered the ward. I gave her all the help I could and she dashed away to join the others without even looking at my feet. When they gathered round she went into her spiel, holding the wrong foot. I jerked my foot about to prove it was in good health, rolled my eyes shook my head but it was no good, she didn't catch on; he let her make a complete fool of herself and then he went for her; she left the ward in tears. He was a miserable bastard; it wasn't her fault he'd been pulled out of retirement.

Every week a number of people were leaving hospital. Some left on crutches and if they were capable of managing for themselves, they were sent home. This constant reshuffling of the beds in the ward led to all the long term cases finishing up together on the one side of the room and that's how I came to know the two Bills. Next to me was young Bill, he was probably in his late forties, old enough to be my father but next to him was old Bill, he could have been my great granddad he looked ninety. Old Bill was totally paralysed and could only make croaking sounds with his throat; young Bill had learned to translate these sounds into

199

old Bill's needs and was a great help to the nurses. Young Bill was also paralysed but his voice was clear; he was propped up in bed every morning, his useless arms resting on pillows and we talked non-stop. The only interruptions were bedpans, medication and feeding. By comparison with the two Bills, I had nothing wrong with me. My bedside companion had been the stage manager of a Liverpool theatre before the war and he was a first class raconteur. I listened fascinated by his stories about all the entertainment personalities he had met, stars like Gracie Fields, George Robey, Rob Wilson and big Bill Campbell and his Liverpool cowboys. I questioned the Liverpool cowboys' existence and my new friend explained.

"Big Bill wasn't going to pay for a dozen extra people on his payroll so he would recruit local lads."
According to the billing, they were all from Texas and when he finished his grand tour he would go back home to Canada. Such insider information was fascinating to me who still believed everything the newspapers said. The therapy girls paid as much attention to him as they did to me and he had faith which must have paid off. Months after I left the hospital and was earning my living again, I had a letter from him. It was an amazing document (regrettably lost in a fire) which he had written using a large piece of paper and holding the pencil with two hands. In readable scrawl he had written, "I am much better and I'll soon be back in show business."

The dedication by the physiotherapy department is something I'll never forget. The girls worked on my knee several times a day increasing the movement one degree at a time. I would have tried to walk but the Thomas splint extended past my foot, so it had to be the wheelchair, when I could borrow one as they were in short supply.

I had accepted the fact that nobody was going to make

my hand look better, it didn't look as sore as before but the skin still had ridges and when I shook hands with anyone they pulled a face like I had leprosy or something. The sister wasn't interested but a young nurse took up my case.

"I think we should treat it like warts and burn it off." This was ok by me,

"Don't ask permission, just do it," I said.

She quietly got on with it and every day she rubbed it with a stick that had some acid on it and gradually the excess skin disappeared. I know my hand was a low priority in a hospital that was up to the limit in disfigured bodies so I was very grateful to this nurse for using her initiative. The ward sister was something else though, I never got any attention from her until the day I caught scabies.

I had been scratching myself for a few days when one morning I noticed the telltale marks between my fingers. I recognised the signs immediately after that bother in Italy a year ago; I was an expert.

"Nurse, I've got scabies."

My confident shout had the nurse believing there was no doubt about it so she fetched the sister. The old cow stood at the bottom of my bed and said,

"Don't be bloody ridiculous, how can you get scabies in my ward?" She wouldn't even take a look.

"I don't know but I've got them, look."

"I used to be a skin sister and I know you can't get scabies in here."

Only an old cow like her could be so confident. She was so adamant and everyone bowed to her superior knowledge. I showed it to the junior doctors but they wouldn't buck the sister's decision so I scratched away in despair. How could the sister be so pig-headed? Scabies is very infectious and I could give it to the whole ward. When the Regiment had had an out-break the MO had been so concerned that he had given us lectures and showed us pictures so we could take action before it spread out of control, so I was very sure of my ground.

Finally, one junior doctor came to see me.
"What makes you think you've got scabies? Why are you so sure?"
"I don't think, I know I have."
I must have impressed her so she gave me more attention.
"I've never seen a case before, so I'm not sure."
I stuck my hand in front of her face and said, "Well you have now."
She gave me a thoughtful look and said,
"I'll see you later when Sister's off duty."

Off she went leaving me with a ray of hope. I had no idea how I had become infected but there had been an outbreak in the 1940s in the country and my connection with it abroad must have had something to do with it; the Sister though wasn't interested in any of this, my hope lay with the younger staff.

At about 7pm that night, the doctor turned up with a wheelchair.
"Can you get into this?"
I was only too glad to. She took me through the hospital grounds to her quarters, a tiny room with a single bed and a table. On that table was a large brass microscope and I knew at once that that was the reason why I was there; she had the edge on all her colleagues.
"Daddy bought it for me when I got my degree."
She fiddled with the lens and said,
"Put your hand under here," I did as I was told.
As she bent over the eyepiece, she gave a gasp of surprise,
"Oh yes, you should see these things." She was so excited.
I was home and dry and I intended to milk the situation

for all its worth.

"I know what they look like, I've seen blown up pictures of them six inches square. Now what about that bloody sister?"

She pushed me back to the ward telling me that now she had something definite, she was going to confront the old dragon. That suited me fine and I hoped that I would be in at the kill. That's not the way it worked out though; the medical profession does not wash its dirty linen in front of the patient.

The following morning, before the ward was awake, two young nurses came for me.

"We're going to treat you in the bath house, get in the chair."

I sat naked in the huge cast iron tub and one of the girls started to paint my hands and feet with a blue dye.

"Could you try to stand up if we put a bar over the bath?"

With my iron leg outside the bath levelling me up and hanging on to the bar, I pulled myself straight. The other nurse had a go with the paintbrush; hands and feet are one thing but the other areas! Well no matter how hard I tried to keep my mind in neutral, it was impossible: I got an erection. The nurse painted away trying to keep a dispassionate face, but soon enough she started to giggle.

"Better lock the bathroom door in case Sister looks in," she said to her mate.

"But I want Sister to see these scabies," I protested.

"Yes but we don't want her to see anything else do we?"

Not knowing what their orders were in delicate matters like this I let the matter drop. I'll get Sister at a less erotic time. They took me back to my bed and Bill was awake and wanted to know what all the laughing was about; I didn't tell him the whole story. The next morning it was the same routine but the original nurse had a different mate with her. On the third day two new nurses came. It must have been disappointing for them to clear up the infection so quickly and I hope it wasn't too disappointing for them when they discussed me in their tea break. I still had no apology from the Sister, so every time she came into the ward, I waved my blue hands at her but she chose to ignore me. I felt like shouting at the top of my voice 'skin sister my arse'. My more mature friend in the next bed convinced me to let the matter drop.

"You're a lot better off than we are, look at old Bill."

Revenge is sweet but you have to be practical and there were other things going on, like the monthly theatre show. I didn't want to be barred from that. Someone was always detailed to push our wheelchairs to the theatre. Young Bill had to be strapped in but he thoroughly enjoyed himself and gave us plenty of technical comment on how the show was put together. Old Bill never had the opportunity to take part; talking or showing him anything never got the slightest reaction or movement. He was just a vegetable making funny noises reminding us that things could be a lot worse. Bill and I were getting ready for the afternoon show, the chair handlers were patients like ourselves and they came to help us. I told the more able one to look after Bill as I could handle my own chair but he had his orders and there were steps outside to negotiate, so we all went to the show together.

Chairs were parked in single file between the banks of seats in the auditorium, then the minders left us to find their own seats. After the show the minders would wait until the audience had cleared then take us back to the ward. One this occasion the chairs in front of me had all gone and I looked round for my help. I couldn't see him anywhere, maybe he thought I didn't need him which was largely true but I had to give him the benefit of the doubt, so I delayed moving out. I was alone in the auditorium so I gave up waiting and started moving towards the door just as it crashed open. I froze as all the mad people rushed in. Nobody had told us that this was the normal practice after every show. As a special treat the original inmates of the hospital were allowed into the theatre to collect all the cigarette ends left by the troops. It was a prize worth fighting for and they rushed about tipping up all the seats and crawling about the floor.

Nobody knew about this event because they were not allowed in until an hour after the show had finished. Someone had blundered and here I was up to my neck in lunatics. In the rush to get to the seats first, no one took any notice of me so I moved slowly down the aisle towards the door that was still open: I didn't get there. Someone grabbed the chair, spun it round and pushed me back up the aisle. This created a new centre of interest and I soon had a crowd. My mind was racing about how to deal with it and the main concern was my iron leg which stuck out straight in front of me like a battering ram. I held on to the wheels but my hands were not strong enough to stop the backward and forward movement that developed as they pushed forward and back like some insane tug of war. When they discovered they could spin the chair, I panicked and lashed out violently. I was getting lessons here that psychiatric nurses had to deal with all the time. Some of them backed off, frightened, others stood back and stared but some took an aggressive attitude; these were my main concern.

At the back of the theatre there were fire doors and I was close enough to make a try for them. With my leg out in front I couldn't just bash into them, I had to get sideways on so that I could lift the emergency bar. With another violent out-burst I managed to get along side the door. As soon as the bar lifted the door swung open and I was out in the corridor. Several of the inmates came out so I made off as fast as I could. I didn't think that any of these loonies would want to leave the rich pickings in the theatre but one of them did and he chased after me. I was pretty handy with a wheelchair but not quick enough to get away from the man who thought I was more interesting than cigarette ends. He grabbed the back of the chair and stopped me dead. He was a big bloke with an insane look on his face, which ruled out any thoughts of using bully tactics. Holding on to the wheels didn't stop him from turning me round and heading back to the theatre. This part of the hospital was unknown to me and when we passed the fire doors I could still hear the commotion inside. I tried to get him to go back inside by making smoking signs but he was not interested and his stupid grin now seemed to have menace. This part of the building was higher than where I came in so I was expecting stairs. Concentrating my mind was my vulnerable left leg and I made a determined effort to stop him going any further but he was too strong.

Just then there was a shout from behind, I turned in the chair and saw a white coated figure waving from the theatre. My cry for help galvanized him into action and he ran towards us. My grinning minder was just as determined to get away but wouldn't let go of the chair and my hands were getting sore trying to slow him down. The attendant seemed to be carrying a club and I shouted for him to be quick. When he caught up with us I could see that his club was a tightly rolled up news paper with which he slapped the head of my loony mate. Then I witnessed as classic a bit of manhandling as I have ever seen. The attendant was a lot smaller than Smiler but with expert use of his 'club', he forced his quarry up against the wall. I watched in amazement as this little man frog-marched the big guy along the corridor to another door. He opened it, pushed his captive through, shut it, then turned to me and said,
"Where do you want to get to, son?"
Relieved, I replied,
"Anywhere outside will do fine."

We had an interesting chat about the history of the hospital. My saviour had worked for the hospital for a long time and on the way back to the ward, he told me the history of the place. The Three Counties Asylum was built in 1860 because an Act of Parliament decreed that the mentally ill should be better treated. The horror stories about places like Bedlam were well known and the Victorians wanted to improve their image. It was set up to provide for Idiots, Lunatics and Imbeciles; anyone of those titles could apply to me. My new friend was a mine of information and went on to tell me about shell shock in the 1914-18 war. Apparently, shell shock was very controversial at first and soldiers were accused of cowardice and Court Martialled. After it was recognised as a form of lunacy, they were admitted to hospital and the Three Counties Asylum became involved with the military as it still was in 1940. I like to think that we were in this place for broken bones not head cases but there were always the nightmares so perhaps we were under more observation than we thought. My carer took me back to the ward and I introduced him to young Bill but I noticed that he was paying attention to old Bill, so maybe we were in the right place after all. Incidentally in these more enlightened times we refer to shell shock as being bomb happy!

The weeks rolled by and the rumours about the war ending were gathering pace. I had just been told that the 56th Division had entered Venice. It was already March 1945 so it had been slow progress, which meant a lot of dying had been going on. We had not had a mention in the newspapers, we were not in Europe so we didn't count. Not that any of this should have interested me, I had also been told that I was to be officially discharged from the Army with a 75% disability pension which was about £2 per week; to get 100% disability pension I would have had to lose the whole leg.

It seemed to me that I was going to be in hospital for ever. I now had about ten degrees of movement in my knee and I thought that I could walk with crutches if they would take the iron off but that was not possible because my foot was still just hanging there. Some people got moved to make it more convenient for visitors but that didn't bother me, I didn't get any. My parents were given free railway warrants but they never used them. That was no surprise to me. Two years later when I got married, my new wife found out about it and she wouldn't have anything to do with them after that. Holding the record for receiving no mail and having no visitors was so unusual that everyone noticed and that gave me a sort of inverted pleasure. I say no visitors, but I did have three at the Three Counties, it's almost poetic is it not? Two of them were sailors. I don't know how they found out where I was because I didn't know them very well but they went to the same school. They were stationed at Malvern and got permission from their superiors to pay me a flying visit on some cock and bull story. Initiative was still rife in the ranks. To be stationed at Malvern so far from the sea showed they had a lot of luck. They spent as little time with me as possible so that they could get on with the real reason for the visit, whatever that was!

The only other visitor I had was the result of a classic encounter worthy of any romantic novel. I had been able to get outside with my wheelchair and since the weather was good, I made off down the long drive to the country lane at the bottom. This was forbidden territory to any patient without a chaperon. As I turned off the drive and onto the road, I saw a horse and cart up ahead going in the same direction. I quickly caught up and swinging out to overtake, I shouted out,
"Move over, you are holding up one of Churchill's broken boys."
The buxom Land Army Girl (LAG) looked down and

said, "Road hog. What ward are you in?"

I screamed back the number and raced on. After
about a mile I stopped, hoping that she would catch
up but she must have turned off into a field so I made
my way back to the hospital. My original plan was to
go to Letchworth which was just up the road but seven
or eight miles in a wheel-chair is not 'just up the road',
it would take too long and I would be missed. So I
gave it no more thought and went back.

Two days later, there was a commotion in the ward
and I heard a voice say,
"I'm looking for the road hog," and there she was with
a huge basket of fruit. I called her over and she sat
on the bed and introduced herself as Ruby. We talked
with the whole ward watching and waiting for me to
hand out the fruit. She told me that there were dozens
of LAGs around the area, that their uniform was not
very flattering with jodhpurs and cowboy hats and
only those with the best figures could get away with
it; but this plump young lady with a great personality
was a joy to be with.

The next serious encounter with the opposite sex was
Mavis. For me this was the real thing but it didn't
work out. Mavis was a Red Cross nurse. The Red
Cross was, and still is, a voluntary service and their
nurses were not subject to the same discipline as the
regular staff. They were able to wear their own shoes
and stockings and even a sensible amount of makeup. Their white dresses with the big red cross on the
front made them look like crusaders from ancient
times. A blue and red cape which was topped off
with a most unpractical headpiece so full of starch
they crackled when they walked past, it made them
very sexy. Mavis was all of this, with a beautiful face
and figure to match. In the parlance of street talk,
Mavis was a posh bird; we were both nineteen and I
was besotted with her. One morning there she was;

she didn't seem to have any real medical duties, just fetched and carried and I monopolized her as much as I could.

Two years after the war when I married, I told my wife about her. My wife had also been in the Red Cross during the war but she said she hadn't been so lucky; it was all bedpans and changing dirty curtains for her. I couldn't imagine Mavis doing anything as sordid as that. We were together on every opportunity either sitting on my bed talking or her pushing me round in the chair. The pictures in Letchworth were favourite and it meant a trip on the bus. Getting the chair on the bus was a problem though; they didn't fold up like modern ones so I would have to stay on the platform with Mavis holding on to me. Everyone stared but I think it was with envy not sympathy. I am sure that she had some feelings for me beyond the nurse and patient routine and my watchful ward mate young Bill, agreed. When they removed my splint, a boot would hold my foot up enough for me to use crutches but it was still awkward because it was not high enough, even so, it meant that Mavis and I could now walk side by side. I know that falling in love with your nurse is a well known cliché but I was sure this was it. One morning she didn't show up and I made frantic enquires but got nowhere. The other nurses simply said,
"She's not a professional, she could be anywhere."

To make matters worse for my love life, they made a special boot with a spring fitted from the toe to the upper part of my leg. Within a few days I was walking without crutches, I was almost a normal person, if only Mavis would show up; but we never met again.

The spring on my foot gave me a limp and my leg was very tired after a short walk but other than that I could see no reason why I should stay in hospital any longer now that Mavis was no longer an incentive. Young Bill tried to cheer me by saying,

"If you had proposed to her you could not have got down on one knee."

He was right about that.

With a 20% bend in my left leg and a stiff and useless index finger on my right hand, I thought that I should nevertheless be able to cope with the outside world. Spirits were very high in the ward because the end of the war was expected in a matter of weeks.

Then I received a devastating letter from Woody's mother, it was dated the 18th of April 1945; my pal had died from his wounds in hospital. The letter I had sent him from Bari hospital had eventually arrived with his effects. His mother must have been shocked by its content. It was written on the assumption that he would survive, such was my faith in the system. The letter didn't say when he died or how long he lasted in hospital, I can only guess. I have read that letter many times since that day and every time I read it, I try to interpret a little more of what it doesn't say. After four years of war, hundreds of mothers had received the dreaded telegram and had to deal with it in their own way. The letter went on to say that she was glad I was doing well and that the Padre had written to her saying that Arthur was a good boy and that had died for God and his County. Well, I knew Woody better that the Padre and he had died because he couldn't stand the stink of a rotting carcass so he had moved up wind. I had stayed put and had survived. It had nothing to do with God and County; it was just bad luck. I could tell none of this to his mother; the Padre's version was better so I never replied to her.

My discharge from the Three Counties Hospital in the spring of 1945 came with plenty of welfare information. The Government was anxious to avoid a repetition of the Great War when dozens of limbless men were begging on street corners and thousands of ex-Servicemen were out of work.

29 JAMES. ST
WEST END
STOKE
STAFFS

Dear Albert,   18·4·45

Thank you very much for your letter I am very glad you and Arthur were pals but I regret to say that Arthur died from Wounds.

We had an Air-mail from is Chaplain and he said that Arthur was a good boy which we already no but that is not haveing him with us but there are alot boys that have died fighting for the Country they love and

The letter from Woody's mum telling me that he had died from his wounds in Italy six months earlier. I was devastated.

have left no one at home
to look after there mother, so I
think that I should not take
it to badly. after all I
have an other son fighting
for the same thing and
I've got a little daughter
and husband to look after.
Well Albert I am very glad
to hear from you and I
hope that you have got
over your wounds alright
and I sincerly hope that
you get on fine at your
place of work.
    I must close now so
Good-bye and Good luck oto
you and thanks for your
letter. Yours sincerly
                        Mrs Wood

Chapter 18

Medals don't count

It was made quite clear to me that my old firm had to give me my job back and allow me to go to hospital twice a week without loss of pay. It was a happy time for most people but I had mixed feelings. I had joined the Forces because there was a war on but now that it was over, I was back living at home. I would have preferred to celebrate the end of the war in the hospital ward with the two Bills. Our goodbyes were inadequate considering the time we had been together but the hospital was under pressure to do the right thing, get people home to their 'loved ones'.

I was at least made welcome by the neighbours. There was bunting across the street from house to house, not from our house of course and there were invitations to parties. I was treated like a local hero and it was very gratifying. Those that knew me well enough would say that I was a bloody fool because there was no need for me to have gone in the first place. They didn't know that if I hadn't been a physical wreck I would have stayed in the Army. With hindsight, by the time the Korean War came round I would have had rank and responsibility. Instead, I was going down to the Labour Exchange to talk about my old job.

The Welfare Officer at the hospital had never been in the real world. I knew they had to give me my job back but wages were negotiable and who could blame them for putting up a fight. I had left as a boy on less than one pound per week. I had learned nothing that was any good to a factory and here I was talking like a man about proper wages, and they had to release me two mornings every week for hospital treatment. All the Labour Exchange could say was, 'you've still got your pension': all that hero stuff had gone out of the window, this was business. The next step was the hospital department where they would give me Faraday treatment for the next two years and finally how much was I going to pay for my bed and board. My parents had not saved any of the money I sent them, two shillings a day for three years. It was a forlorn hope that they might have saved the money for me, what would I do with £109 quid. None of these issues were settled to my satisfaction but in order to get on with life I didn't make a fuss, my time would come.

In due course I went round to my old factory where I had started in 1940. I left the bus and walked down Holdford Road, a typical street born in Birmingham's industrial past. Entrances to several factories, a scruffy shop and the rest made up of terraced housing. By Higgs' Motors, I stopped and smiled, I know a story about Higgs; in fact I know two stories, mine and my uncle's.

My uncle Dick, after being gassed in the Great War, left hospital and got a job at the HP Sauce factory. He was working there when I was born, he seemed to have been there forever and I remember my dad telling me what terribly low wages he got. He worked in the packing department and wooden cases had to have wire around them, so there was always plenty of scrap off cuts of wire about. My uncle kept chickens and took a six inch piece of wire to tie up the pen door. He made it into a loop and put it on the handle bars of his bike; no attempt was made to hide it. At the end of the day and on his way out of the factory, the gate-keeper stopped him and demanded to know where the wire came from. My bewildered uncle told him and he was marched back inside and charged with theft.

When the case came to court, the Magistrate was amazed that a man with such a good record should be brought before him and he tried to determine the value of the wire. The wire was bought in two ton coils at less than £3 per coil, so unless you used scales that could weigh grams, it was impossible to calculate. Nevertheless, the law had been broken so the Magistrate fined my uncle one penny and then rebuked the firm for wasting his time. Of course, my uncle was sacked and so he started to work at Higgs' Motors, still on lousy wages.

My story is different; in the Army I was canon fodder, in civilian life I was factory fodder. For my first job after leaving school, they sent me to Higgs'. I turned up, all washed and brushed and they sat me in an office then ignored me for hours. A young chap came in and asked me what I was waiting for, I told him and he said, "You don't want to work here, it's a lousy place. Go next door, they pay better."
I was still mulling over what he had said when someone decided to come and deal with me. I stood up and said, "Don't bother," and walked out.
Next door the factory made mudguards and they paid me one shilling a week more, not a very intelligent way to start a career.

When I stood outside my old factory in 1945, I was not a 'green kid' anymore. I had a few talents that they wouldn't like to know about, not that they would help me in here. I walked though the gate and the first person I saw was Mac, the timekeeper; he has been in the same job all through the war. Nobody liked Mac; I remembered he had a habit of closing the gates in your face dead on eight o'clock then making you wait half an hour before he opened them again. When I was there before as a kid, Mac did it once too often to a lorry driver, the driver pulled him half way through the little window until he was stuck. I knocked on the same little window, he opened it and looked at me. "Hello Mac, still locking them out?"

He didn't recognise me so I handed my Labour

216

Exchange papers over. The window was so small it was like ordering a meal at a Chinese take-away.

Still peering at me suspiciously, he said, "Take them up to the office."

I didn't go to the office. I decided to have a look round the factory first. Mudguards had given way to aircraft parts and there were a lot of unfamiliar machines about.

The tool room was my next port of call. About eight men worked in there in the old days and there were bound to be a lot of changes. There were. It was crowded but I saw some familiar faces, people whom I had worked with before. They gathered round and asked the usual questions.

"Did you see any action?"

"Did you kill anybody?"

I held my own with their morbid queries then I saw the tool room foreman nearby, he didn't seem to have changed.

I shouted, "Hello Fred," he looked across and said, "Come to the office when you've done."

In the tool room office there was a bloke I knew very well, Joe Green, "Hello Joe, I'm looking for Fred Pulley."

He was surprised to see me and asked me some intelligent questions. He was a quiet chap and the butt of a lot of jokes because he looked so untidy. His cow gown was always patched with different coloured material, he was nicknamed the 'prisoner of war' by the lads. Without enlightening me about any changes he took me round to see Pulley. I knocked on the door and entered.

"You shouldn't come in until I say so, sit down over there." His tone was unpleasant and before I could make any response he started in on me.

"Before we go any further let's get one thing straight, it's not Fred anymore, it's Mr Pulley."

I was taken aback, five minutes before a crowd of

people were treating me like a hero, now there was this guy treating me like shit. I was speechless as he went on,

"I'm the general manager now just remember that."

I got up and stood in front of his desk; there were some heavy items on the top of it and he never knew how close he was to having his face smashed in. A little voice in my head said, "keep control, you're not in the back streets of Cairo now."

I turned and made for the door, "Ok," I said.

"Ok Mr Pulley," he shouted, "and see Mr Green, he'll fix you up."

I went out and leaned against the wall, this was a bad start to the day.

It was typical of Joe Green not to tell me that he was the tool room foreman; he didn't look the part, no white coat or attitude to match.

"Pulley has just been laying down the law to me," I said, "I don't think I'm going to like it here."

Joe was reassuring and tried to explain what a tough time they had had over the last four years, eighty hours a week, no sleep because of the bombing and fire watch on the factory roof three times a week. He made me feel like I'd had it easy. There was a lot of truth in what he said; civilians in major cities had been in more danger than 50% of the Forces overseas. I had to rely on Joe for the next twelve months to cover for my obvious lack of experience and I shall always be in his debt but I was able to do him a favour some years later.

The factory was not my only problem; my nightmares had come back. There had been very few during the last months in hospital but now, shouting in the middle of the night and wetting the bed didn't help my relationship with my stepmother. It didn't stop there, certain noises would make me perspire and on one occasion the screaming wheels on a trolley caused me to instinctively react by throwing myself to the factory floor. I tried to explain it away to the surprised people who saw me by saying that I had tripped up. To add to my difficulties I had no choice but to live at home, I could not afford to live anywhere else. Twice a week at the hospital I tried to explain and they put me on medication but progress was slow.

In April everyone expected the end of the war to be announced. Mussolini had been caught by the mob and hung on a lamppost in Milan. He had been in power longer than Hitler which brought the Italian campaign back into the news briefly. I poured over the maps to find out where our lads would finish up when the end came. Everyone wanted their lads to come home but my feelings were more complex. I would have been considered very weird to say I wished I was back there with them; it was just the opposite for most people. If I had not been injured I saw myself ending up in some mercenary force in some other part of the world. There was plenty of choice and the pay was very attractive considering the three shillings a day I had been getting.

Dorothy was my friend before I went overseas; I had even sent her a cameo from Naples. I had never considered Dorothy a serious girlfriend because she didn't want it that way but now I was keen to pursue the affair further. I had been home a few days and decided that it was time for me to call. When I arrived at her house arrangements were being made for a street party and I helped move folding tables about. When we had a chance to be alone I showed her my tattoos, having her name on my arm did not impress her one bit.
"That was a silly thing to do, what if you meet someone else?" She obviously still did not intend to be that someone. I was so keen on this girl that I had to persevere and when she said she went to a Saturday dance with friends I invited myself.

The Palace Ballroom was strictly for dancing, soft drinks only and a sprung floor. I was pretty good at dancing and I didn't suffer from shyness like most kids. I was full of confidence and once the music started I was straight out on to the floor. I should have accepted that things would be different since my encounter with an 88mm shell but I had to learn the hard way. I was clumsy, gauche and inept. My partner kept catching her shoe on my leg brace and her friends were laughing at me. Swank and style were the order of the day so I retired to the bar and stared viciously at my glass of lemonade. That was the end of dancing with Dorothy and I forgot to ask her if she ever got my cameo from Naples. After one more brief visit I never saw her again, I hope she lived happily ever after.

I now had enough movement in my knee to ride a bicycle, with difficulty. This was excellent exercise and soon I could cycle with the best of them, even with the leg brace. The end of the war was announced early in May and enough has been written about that event; I shall not dwell on it except to say that during the celebrations I met Alice. Alice was a beauty and she knew it. A friend of hers told me that even at school her mother had vetoed physical training lessons because it messed up her hair! Showing her off to all my friends gave me a big head. Her mother was a widow and she doted on me and fed me several times a week; my feet were well and truly under her table. It lasted for a month and then the bombshell. One night Alice opened the door and said, "I'm sorry, I've made other arrangements." I was shattered. "But what about these," I was holding up two tickets for a show on Saturday night.
"Try and get your money back," and she closed the door.

I could have gone over her head and appealed to mom but they were close and must have talked it over. I got on my bike and pedalled away. I didn't wish her happy ever after but I did find out the reason for my humiliation. Alice had met a guy with a sports car, I saw them in it, it was red. I felt a lot better after that, to lose out to red sports car put things in the right perspective. Going after a girl on a bicycle was not an option, I had to get myself some decent wheels.

There are people who boast about being the first one in their family to have a university education, so what? I was the first one in my family to be motorized. When I was a kid, nobody in the entire district had a car; you could swank about it even if you only knew somebody with one. Anyone born in the 1920s could never dream that far ahead, I was about to break the mould. I admit a car was a little over the top but what about a motorcycle? I got one for £17, more than two months wages. Boadicea couldn't have been more proud if she had gone up our road in her chariot, I was 'Jack the lad' in spades. Life's lessons are very expensive at £17 a time, the bike turned out to be rubbish. No new machines were made during the war years, old bangers were turning up for sale on street corners and bombsites all over the city. You had to be careful and I got it right the second time; I was now a bona fide motorcyclist, the girls came free and easy and the pillion was always occupied.

Swank played a big part in youth culture in those days and one stunt was to tell the girls that you had your name down for a new car. It didn't matter, there was a two year waiting list and if the car became available you sold your place to someone who could afford to pay for it. The dealers put paid to that one by asking for a deposit. Another ruse was to buy an ex-Army machine. When the dealers sold these bikes on, they were re-registered, so the log book said it was a 1946 model and that meant it was new; all the girls believed that one. The dealers were on to a good thing by buying from the military at less than £5, spraying over the camouflage paint and selling on at £50. Mine was a 350cc Enfield, painted maroon, paid for at ten shillings a week on the knock, it served me well.

One of my biker friends was also a workmate called Doug Murray. He was two years older than I was and because of his reserved occupation, he was never called up. He was also a very good toolmaker and was paid a lot more money. Doug bought a dream machine, a Triumph Speed Twin. In 1946, it was the ultimate in motorcycles and it was a pleasure to cruise alongside him on the road. We had a lot of adventures together, Blackpool in four hours, Weston-super-Mare in two and Barmouth, on the Welsh coast, in one and a half hours. What with the age, money and the bike, Doug was very much my senior which meant he got the best girl as well.

Doug had a brother named Henry, also a biker. Occasionally he joined us but when he did there was trouble. Henry was an extrovert; one day an attractive woman in a flash car knocked him off his bike: Henry lay in the road completely unhurt. The concerned woman rushed over to him whereupon Henry said that if she didn't fix a date with him, he would scream with pain. Another time we all went to the big Onion Fair at Witton. We paid our shilling to watch the Wall of Death riders whiz around the wooden cylinder, our heads looking down over the top. The first rider went round towing a scantily dressed woman on roller skates behind him. Then she disappeared and another rider appeared; they then both raced round in fake competition. After the show the proprietor stood in the centre, looked up and told us that it was so dangerous they couldn't get insurance and any extra coins would be appreciated. Half crowns and two shilling pieces rained down on him like a thunderstorm.

Henry had something to say, loudly. "Dangerous my arse, it's fuckin' easy."

The coins stopped showering down, a circle of faces stared at the three of us; Doug and I edged away from Henry trying to convey to the others that we were not together. The ringmaster looked up, he couldn't let this pass.

"If you think it's easy, you want to try it mate."

"Right," shouted Henry, "I'll be down in the bat of an eye," and he was off.

"He's the one who is bats," said Doug. "We had better go after him, he can be crazy."

We found Henry banging on the small door in the wooden wall; after an age the door opened two inches and a voice said,

"For God's sake go away until I've cleaned up in here."

Henry wouldn't leave it at that, so we left him to it and enjoyed the rest of the fair. That wasn't the end of the Wall of Death, on Sunday morning Doug came round to tell me that his brother had fixed up to have a go while the fair was closed, he was already on his way. We raced over as quickly as possible but when we got there Henry had already been round the wall several times.

"I told you it was easy, all you have to do is stay under the white line. There is a tendency to go upwards when you speed up; about 20 to 25mph is all that's needed. I couldn't use my own bike because the carburettor has to be set different or it runs out of fuel."

There were actually only two riders in the show, when the girl in tights put on her leathers, it gave the impression that there were three.

"He's offered me a job, said Henry, "the money's fabulous."

We didn't know what to say.

"Are you going to take it?" Doug enquired,

"I'm going to think about it seriously."

The next time I met Henry, I heard the reason he didn't take the job.

"He wanted me to share a caravan with that other

rider. He was filthy and lived like a pig."
"What about the bird?" I asked,
"She shared with the proprietor, it was out of bounds.
The boss had made that very clear."
Anyway, Henry liked his creature comforts and had a
very good mum. I wish I could have said the same.

I had been working for about three months when
I was called before a Pension Revue Board. Three
gentlemen sat on the other side of the table: the one
in the middle was Lord somebody or other and he was
doing the talking.
"I see that you haven't lost any time off work Mr
Darlington?"
All the time he was talking I was thinking, how do
you address this pratt. M'lord? Your Grace? Your
Worship or just plain Sir? In the event I didn't use any
of them.
"No, because the pay is so low I can not afford to. I go
to work in pain." Did I detect a glimmer of a smile?
Maybe not; he went on,
"But you are doing the same job as you did before your
injuries."
This guy was probably a hard working civil servant
but I was not old enough to understand that kind of
mature thinking yet. To me he was the enemy and I
had to have a go.
"No I'm not. I can't do such heavy tools as I did before.
Look at this hand, I can't grip anything."
His face was expressionless as he said,
"That will be all Mr Darlington."

Two weeks later, they reduced my pension from 75%
to 50%. I don't think that it would have made any
difference if I had called him M'lord; this latest blow
only highlighted my already poor wage.

Now that Christmas was out of the way, 1946 was
going to be a challenge. I had two major problems:
living at home and poor wages. At work, no matter

how hard I tried, I would always be the 'kid' but going outside and calling myself a toolmaker was a huge risk. On the other hand, the Birmingham Mail had columns of vacant situations for toolmakers night after night. What could be the worst scenario: I could move to another firm, they could find out that I'm crap and they could give me the sack. No big deal: I was sure of myself on most machines but there were some technical mysteries that I wasn't happy about, in other words the matrix of the business. I should have to pick my next place of work with care. I am not an egalitarian; if I work harder than the next man, I want more money for my effort.

During these uncertain times, I even discussed starting a window cleaning round with another old school friend. He had been discharged from the Navy and was looking and hoping like the rest of us. We sat on the grass verge and discussed the difficulties of getting £25 capital and a ladder: it stumped us. We did some work on the bombed buildings instead. He got the sack for repairing a roof with tiles from the house next door that wasn't damaged. There were people living there and they came into the works office in a very wet and excited state. I was working on mortise joints for window frames at the time and watched them screaming at the boss. Neither my friend nor I were cut out for this kind of caper. About fifteen years later, when I was established, I moved to another factory and let him have my old lease. He made a success of it and moved to very modern premises and became the well known 'Maurice Walker Tools Limited'. The lesson here is stick to what you know best, it's the only way.

Chapter 19

Cheap at the price

The Jewellery Quarter in Birmingham is famous for its fine art, sweat shops and ruined property. I stood outside one such place and wondered if the bombing had caused the mess. They certainly knew how to get the most out of Victorian buildings: kitchens became tool rooms, dinning rooms became press shops, bedrooms became offices and even the outside loo became a stores. Back to back buildings and narrow streets made deliveries a nightmare but somehow it all worked. There were a lot of precious metals about but security didn't seem to be a problem either.

I was about to find out more of this strange world because the bloke I was talking to was going to give me a job. I had to get the job first though before I told him that I had to go to the hospital twice a week. When I did, he had a shock but I pointed out that it wouldn't cost him as I would make up the hours lost. I figured it would take a real miserable bastard to go back on his word after that. After all, I was one of Churchill's broken boys; he conceded and I was in my first real job on a proper wage.

The main reason which put toolmakers at the top of the list of artisans, was the accuracy of their workmanship for which they were famous. Use of the micrometer, vernier and sine bar made them the elite. There was no evidence of that at this firm; the boss was only interested in how cheap he could make the component which might be part of an earring or the clasp for a bracelet. Nobody seemed to make a finished piece of jewellery; everyone just made bits for somebody else. We used the cheapest tool steel, some rubbish called half and half because one side was iron and the other side was carbon steel. The boss did all the hardening himself in a gas muffle, which was expensive to run but it enabled him to use a bit of psychological pressure. He would come up to you all nice and smiling and say that Jack would have his die ready by Wednesday, could you have yours ready at the same time because putting them both in together saved a lot of expense. That meant breaking your back on Tuesday to get it done in time; none of these lessons were wasted on me, when I went into business for myself I invented a few more.

With problem number one out of the way I now had time to concentrate on the second. Living at home meant I had to go out every night of the week, there was no way that I could spend time in the evening with my parents. In the days before universal television, you had to talk in the evenings and we had nothing to talk about. I started at the Central Technical College on a course that took care of two nights a week but we finished at 9pm so it was into the pub for an hour and a half or find a girlfriend with a mum who did evening meals.

Where to live was a problem affecting every one after the war; married couples with children were being told that they would have to wait ten years for a council house. In the private sector, houses built for £300 before the war were now selling for £1500. Doug and I looked for a rented flat but they demanded a high deposit and I could never come up with my end. The answer was to get more money. I had contact with other ex-Servicemen and their answer was taking it off somebody else. I had never considered a life of crime but I had practiced some techniques that would work on a bank or wage office and so had these other three guys. A bank would be a very soft target.
"They don't even shoot back at you," they said.

It was beginning to look good. In the post war climate, there were a lot of weapons about and I wasn't all that surprised to be given a .38 revolver and a handful of bullets. I gave it serious thought but I wasn't up to it physically, if we got into any rough stuff I would let them down and I said so. Twanging about with a spring on my shoe wasn't very practical. They agreed and asked me to drive the car instead. I didn't have to steal a car, we used one belonging to one of the gang. After the job, I was to dump it in a side road and he would report it stolen.

The target they picked was a well-known bookies office. I parked further up the road from the office, I couldn't risk being blocked in by other cars and I had to be moving when they came out onto the street. It all went well except for one thing, their inside information was wrong; there was nowhere near the amount of money expected. My cut was only £200 and I made up my mind that that was the one and only time I would get mixed up in a caper like that. The other lads went on to bigger and more infamous things, getting headlines in the years to come and doing their share of porridge as well!

I kept the gun for years until a chap begged me to let him have a go with it; he had never had the chance to fire anything before. We went into some woods and he used up all the bullets firing into a tree, then he wanted to buy the gun. I agreed to a swap with a Samurai sword that his brother had brought back from Burma. In my study, I have a cabinet full of all kinds of memorabilia; the Samurai is there and so is a Gurkha Kukri knife, to replace the one I lost in Italy: it's all to do with memories . . .

My old mate Harold, from the Avonmouth caper, had finally got into the Navy; he had been discharged and was now back at the old firm. He had the same problem as me.
"I'll always be the kid," he said.
I agreed to try and get him a job with me. My boss

said bring him along to see me. Harold turned up and asked for 3d an hour more than I was getting and he got it. Naturally, I went straight in to see the boss for my increase, but the answer was 'No'. The boss said that Harold had more experience than me because he didn't go into the Navy until 1944. I couldn't argue with that but there was still a lot of choice out there so it was time to move on.

After that, I averaged a job a month always chasing the extra money. There was one amusing incident at a place called Norton Pressing. Five other toolmakers were waiting for an interview. We started chatting and when they heard how many jobs I'd had they suggested that I went in first. The boss had an office which was two floors up, a single flight of stairs went straight up to his door.
With remarks about going up to see God, I set off up the staircase.
"Don't worry, I'll soon find out how heavenly he is," I replied.
The boss sat at his desk with the tool room foreman at his side. He started to talk but I was now an expert at this game so I cut him short,
"What's the rate?" He was irritated and snapped,
"We'll have to see how you shape up."
"Ok, I've shaped up all right, now what's the rate?"
"We do some very tricky work here, we would have to see how you cope with it."
"Ok, I've been here a month and I've done all your tricky stuff, what rate am I on?"
The boss just stared at me so the tool room foreman picked up the ball,
"Some of my men, who have been with me a long time, can earn as much as 1/9d per hour."
I stood up and walked to the door; there was no reaction from them so I closed the door behind me and looked down at the sea of anxious faces. In my best Corporal's voice I said,
"He only wants to pay one and nine pence top whack."

Some walked away at once and I was about six steps down when the boss came out,
"What's going on?" he demanded.
"You want to read the papers and get up to date mate."
I carried on down with a smile thinking of Fred Pulley, by the time I got to the bottom all the others had gone.

I finished up with a job twelve miles out of town. The early morning race at 90mph along a deserted road was a great start to the day and so was the money at the end of the week but the job in the middle was a mistake. The firm, which was owned by an American, repaired combine harvesters, tractors and cranes. They didn't need a toolmaker only someone who could use a lathe, making an endless supply of bronze bearings. None of the hicks there could sharpen a cutter or a drill, so I was continually asked to deal with it. I have never known time drag so much, I was in a time warp and my dissatisfaction didn't impress the Yankee boss either.
"God-dam-it son, I pay you more than the others, so get with it or else."

I had kept in touch with my uncle Dick and aunt Amy and on one of my visits, I met their new lodger. He was a chap my age, down from Scotland and trying for work in the Midlands; we became life long friends. When I told him about my well paid but lousy job, he suggested we go up to Glasgow for a holiday and stay with his parents. My firm operated a flexible holiday scheme so that they wouldn't have to close for a week in August. When I asked the boss for a week's holiday he wasn't very pleased,
"You God-dam Limeys always want something." I offered to do the August stint. He agreed, "Ok, you have your arse back here next Monday morning right on."
I nearly answered, "Affirmative sir."
I told my Scottish mate that we had some logistics

to work out; petrol was rationed and we didn't have enough coupons to do both ways. Doug and I had made it to Blackpool but this was three times as far. "No problem," said Bill, "when we get to Glasgow, my mates will fix us up with coupons."

I thought it would be better if I had a back up plan, so on Saturday night I went back to the firm and climbed over the fence into the yard. I siphoned off two large cans and filled my tank to the top with petrol from the tractors. I had already checked and made sure that they were not using diesel. I figured this firm owed me because they were boring me to death. When we packed the panniers on the bike for the journey up north, I took the siphoning gear just to be on the safe side. As an afterthought, I put the revolver in as well. I don't know what I was thinking of and now it all seems a bit extreme but things were so uncertain at that time.

We made Glasgow in good time and Bill introduced me to his parents, Mr and Mrs O'Brien. Straight off, Mr O'Brien made it clear that he didn't like the English, "All the roads round here were made by Scotsmen under the English whip."
He was referring to General Wade's love of civil engineering in the 18th Century. I apologised as best I could for the General but it did no good, until Sunday. Under Scottish law, as it was at that time, only travellers could get a drink on a Sunday, so what they all did was move down the road to the next village and the good people of that village in turn moved up to yours. Mr O'Brien said he would make sure that we would get our drink; the fact that we were already travellers from Birmingham made no difference to him. On the following Sunday, Bill's dad prepared to show us how to get it done.
"You've got to be travellers or they can refuse to serve you." He laboured the point to make sure we got the picture.

"Ok dad, show us how to do it," said Bill.

We got on a bus to Balloch at the south end of Loch Lomond. After a few pints, O'Brien senior mellowed and I was able to remark what a fine road it was that had brought us to this lovely inn; he didn't take offence and we became friends. He thought that I was different from the other English people he knew because I had heard of Hadrian's Wall and knew about the Black Watch. After that Sunday, I could do no wrong.

I can understand the Scottish attitude towards the English; memories are long and a long succession of English kings, from Edward I on, didn't do them any favours. When in Scotland always refer to the flower Sweet William as Stinking Billy and you can't go far wrong.

There was a lot to see in the Highlands but mindful of the petrol situation we couldn't explore as much as we would have liked. We stayed longer than expected, looking up the high and low life of Glasgow. Finally we had to prepare for the journey home; we had already stayed longer than a week. Bill's mates hadn't come up with any coupons but they did scout around with my siphoning gear and made sure that we started with a full tank but no spare cans. I knew we would have to pinch somebody's petrol before we got to Preston. If you've got to steal, it's better to wait for the dark, so we didn't start out until the afternoon. By the time we cleared Carlisle the weather was bad and getting worse. Bill was concerned about going over Shap Fell in Westmorland, as it was then, in the dark and bad weather; I was only worried about petrol supplies and finding a likely victim.

The garage seemed closed for the night but there were some cars parked on the forecourt and I decided to try my luck. I pulled alongside a vehicle on the offside to the building whilst Bill walked about in the road ready to tip me off if someone started to pull in. As I reached into my pannier, a dog barked and lights came on above the garage; it was a no-no. I pushed the bike silently out into the road and we made off towards Penrith. Bill was still going on about the Shap Fell road. In the days before motorways, some of the mountain roads were a problem and the village of Shap, which stands on the A6 and was the highest main road in England, the M6 at Shap still is, was usually closed when it snowed but this was just bad weather and I had a bigger problem on my mind.

We went through Penrith and over Shap Fell; it was no big deal and we approached Kendal. I motored very slowly keeping a sharp look out. It wasn't the money, petrol was the equivalent of five pence per gallon at today's value, it was the coupons, the ration was very mean and that's what made me behave in this manner. It was midnight and we had passed the built up area of Kendal without any luck. Then a police car overtook us and that put paid to any skullduggery for the moment. I opened up the speed and in another three minutes I would have been doing 65mph and telling a different story but there was an almighty crash and that changed everything.

The bike I was riding had a logbook that said it was registered in 1946 with zero mileage. I knew that was all rubbish, it was an ex-Army bike and God knows how it was treated in the Services. It had the old type of girder forks that had a series of brazed tubes making a box section with a large spring in the centre; it was the brazing that had broken down all one side of the forks. With nothing to connect the front wheel to the main frame, the bottom of the engine had crashed into the road and over we went. Bill was half asleep with his hands jammed in his overcoat pockets for warmth. He went over the top of me and landed on the grass verge on the right hand side of the road. It was an acrobatic miracle that he fell in the sitting position and was not hurt. I had heard the brazing snap but could not react in time; I came out of the seat, went over still holding the handle-bars and lay on my back in front of the bike. We both just sat there in a daze, shaken but unhurt.

The police car came back and stopped between us. The officer got out and looked us over saying,
"I wondered where you two had got to when you didn't pass me further down the road."
He had assumed we must be up to no good; bad luck but there was still something he could do.
"I want you to witness the situation officer, we haven't run into anything and no pot holes in the road either, it happened without any warning."
The Constable agreed with me and said I could use his name and then he spoilt everything by saying,
"You can't stay in the road all night. Come with me, you can sleep in the cells," and because he could see our alarm, he added, "don't worry, I won't lock the door."
It wasn't the door that worried me it was the gun in my pannier bag. If he looked in there it would really make his night. We pushed the bike off the road and collected a bag each, then went with him to Kendal clink. It was a quiet town and we had the cell to ourselves. In the morning he gave us a cup of tea and a piece of toast; he was a nice guy,
"I'm going off duty soon so I'll drop you off so you can sort the bike out."
With some information about trains we did just that.

Kendal railway station was quite a way and we had to lift the front of the bike and push it like a wheelbarrow on the back wheel. There was an early morning train to Birmingham if we could get there in time. The train was already in the station when we got there so we pushed the bike straight on to the goods van, ignoring the protests from the aged porter and went to the ticket office.

Big problem: we hadn't got enough money.

"But it's already on the train"

"Then get it off again, the train leaves in eight minutes."

This guy had his peaked cap on and he wasn't giving an inch.

I said to Bill quietly, "Stall as much as you can, that old guy can't lift the bike off on his own."

I turned back to the ticket window and started an argument; several other people had made a queue.

The ticket man was now shouting at me, "Get it off."

A man in the queue said, "We'll all miss the bloody train at this rate. How much are you short son?"

It was less than two pounds and he handed over two notes.

"Give me your address and I'll send it."

He looked blank, he had already written it off but I made sure that he got it back.

We ran to the train and jumped into the Guard's van, there wasn't time to find seats. The porter had had enough messing about so he shot the sliding door forward and waved the train out. I knew we shouldn't be travelling in the Guard's van but who cares as long as we got there. On the way back to Birmingham, we had time to reflect upon our holiday; it wasn't a complete success but we had had a go. 'Having a go' was a metaphor for a lot of things in post war Britain. Rationing and shortages were making spivs out of us all and pulling a stroke seemed to be the norm. The new Labour Government wasn't doing very well, everything was nearly as difficult as in wartime. Incidentally, I wasn't old enough to vote in 1945 but my papers came based on my Army age, so I did. Nobody could blame me for the landslide Labour victory, I voted for the other side!

It was still morning when we arrived in Brum and so there was plenty of time to get the bike sorted. I had bought the motorbike on the knock from King's of Oxford. It was quite a way from the station so we started pushing straight away and nasty looks from the sales staff didn't deter us from pushing it through their posh showroom.

"What did you run into?" were the manager's opening remarks.

"Nothing," was my reply, "that's why you've got to fix it."

"You're insured aren't you?"

"Only third party."

"That's your problem."

"No mate, it's your problem and I'll tell you why."

I had given this matter a lot of thought and wasn't going to stand for any argy bargy so I laid it on thick about the police constable witness and put words into his mouth,

"He said it was a death trap," and I threatened to telephone Kendal police there and then.

"There's no need for all that, just put it in the workshop at the back," said the salesman.

He climbed down so quickly I should have realized that I had a solid case but I was green so I didn't claim for other losses.

"I'm not paying HP while it's laid up."

"It will be ready in a couple of days."

I came away thinking I had won but with hindsight, the compensation I could have got still grieves me to this day every time I drive down the Bristol Road.

The day was still young so Bill and I took our time round the city centre before we made our way to the bus, the number 5, Perry Common for him and the number 11, Erdington for me.

I arrived home and because it was Saturday afternoon both my boring parents where in. The old man was reading his newspaper and my stepmother sat starring at the table.

"So you're back are you?"

I didn't bother to answer the obvious, so she went on,

"What about this then?

There was a more uncomfortable atmosphere than usual so I paid attention to what she was looking at. There in the middle of the table were my employment cards. The phrase, 'get your cards' was always in the plural because there were two cards, one for medical insurance and one for the old age pension and there were mine, along with a slim wage packet. This was great! On the train coming home the one thing that I had made up my mind about, was to pack in my awful job. The Yankee boss had saved me a lot of trouble. *"That God-dam kid hasn't shown up. Send him his cards."* He had even sent my three days' pay which firms always hold in lieu; they usually made you wait for it. He didn't want me to have any excuse to visit; good for you my old colonial mate, don't stand any nonsense from these God-dam Limeys! My mind, now relieved from the difficulty of getting to work without a motorbike, was able to concentrate on what number two step-mom was going on about,

"You've had the sack, don't expect me to keep you."
Heaven forbid: five years of war and her thinking was still in the past when getting the sack was paramount even to having a baby out of wedlock.
"I'll get another job on Monday."
My father said, "It can't be that easy."
"Of course it is, I've had four jobs I haven't even told you about."
Sure enough on Monday I was fixed up, I can't remember the name of the firm because I gave in my notice before the end of the week.

Doug came to see me with a much better proposition. He had landed a job with a firm that made quality diaries and office files. It was clean work because it used mainly tin-plate so there wasn't the usual oil and muck about. I was impressed.
"Never mind about tin-plate, you should see the fringe benefits," said Doug, "the place is full of young girls on hand presses."
I was doubly impressed.

"There are only four of us in the tool-room and I can get you in." The answer was 'yes' but I needed time to sort out my bike first. Forgoing a hospital visit I went to see the dealer instead.

I had been playing truant from my therapy quite a lot lately and my foot was much improved; I was also leaving the spring off my shoe for several hours a day. King's of Oxford had fixed my bike by putting on forks from another Army bike; they were still in the original camouflage paint. I would have to wait another week for them to be sprayed Maroon. I couldn't wait, so I turned up at Doug's firm on Monday morning on a two-tone motorcycle. There always seem to be balances in life so that you don't get too much luck at any one time; my good fortune was marred by a letter from the Pensions' Board. The subsequent visit to the faceless men left me reduced to 30%: I was now on thirteen shillings and six pence per week, which seemed to be a Government guide line because after that they left me alone for years.

The new firm was every bit as good as Doug had said it was; two large semi-detached houses converted to make one large factory. The tool room had originally been the dining room because there was a serving hatch in the wall. As soon as I settled in, the hatch crashed open and a woman put her head through it.
"Where's the new bloke?" I approached and she said, "Are you on for Friday night?" I looked at Doug for some guidance.
"Fringe benefits," he said.
Every Friday night they had a coach which took them on a mystery tour to some pub in the country.
"Ok," I said.
A hand came through, "Five bob please."
Feeling like an orphan, I confessed to being broke. The hand went back and the hatch slammed shut.
"Don't you go upsetting our Gladys," said one of the blokes.

Doug took over and said, "Take him round and introduce him to some of the talent before Herbert comes in."

I asked who Herbert was, "He's in charge of all the factory floor but he doesn't bother us much in here."

I was taken on a rapid tour upstairs; some of the bedroom walls had been taken down leaving space for a large hand press shop. There were rows of young girls, working and chatting away, all taking an interest in the new bloke. I noticed that some of them were looking down at my lower half; Doug had been telling them lurid tales about my war experience.

There was one room which I was warned about, "Keep out of there," said my tour guide, "it's full of old dears, rough as hell. One of the tool setters fell down the stairs trying to get away, broke his wrist." As an after thought he added, "Gladys is in there." Well you can't have it all, sport.

Down on the ground floor in the power press shop I met Herbert, he seemed all right. I could tell he was a very serious man. I was given a tip about how to handle him.

"Always ask how his family is doing; by the time he's finished showing photographs of the kids, he'll forget what he wanted to bollock you about."

He did remind me to keep my mind on my work. "Some of these roll feed tools are difficult," he said pointing to the production line, "Doug will put you right."

There was no tool room foreman but Doug was the senior hand so we took our orders from him. He was the only one who could make the pressure die cast tools, used on the small expensive loose leaf diaries. Dougie Murray had used his time well whilst I was away at war.

This place suited me fine and I stopped looking at the 'situations vacant' column and settled down to the routine. One of the girls took me home at lunch time and her mother fed me and insisted that I come every day. I knew where that would lead, so I spaced myself out; it was like having a private harem. The Friday night mystery trip put icing on the cake and I never missed one. I did get caught on one occasion; Doug and I, trying to save five shillings, decided to follow the coach on our motor bikes. We landed up at the Bull in Meriden, near Coventry. We had the usual good time and on the way back, while tailgating the coach, one of the girls was sick. She put her head out of the window and it went all over Doug who then swerved into me. Getting killed to save five bob wasn't worth it. The damage to my bike was substantial so I changed it for a Royal Enfield Silver Bullet. It still wasn't as good as Doug's Triumph Speed Twin but it was more up market.

The rest of that year I did very well except that my college course was neglected because of all the other distractions. I never did get a qualification. I realize now how short sighted that was but at the time nobody could have changed my ways. I could be very determined in some things but my flesh was weak. Living at home was now less of a problem as there were so many places where I could stay over night: all I needed were safe houses where I could leave a change of clothes.

Working class morality was still rife in the 1940s, the war had not changed that for everyone. I lived in a street where curtains twitched and neighbours whispered. So much so that my step mom was questioned in the butchers, of all places. I knew the butcher well, he had offered me a job when I left school but he had a son of my age so I knew I would never own the shop. He was a very jolly man and he made matters worse with his interpretation of my activities when he heard the gossip. Step mom two was very embarrassed and told my father, she probably whispered to him. The old man told me about it, but it didn't change anything. I should have charged them a fee for enriching their lives!

Doug and I still had no luck trying to find a flat and now he was talking about emigration, Canada, South Africa and Australia were all looking for white skilled tradesmen. Australia was offering to take you for only £10 but Doug was stuck on South Africa. A lot of Servicemen had sailed round Africa to get to the Far East because the Mediterranean was closed to the British for the first two years of the war. They all said how hospitable it was in Cape Town, so it was all right by me. We made enquiries and came up against a snag, at least I did, money. Apart from the boat fare, you had to put up bond money. If you were no good they could ship you back home at no cost to themselves. I didn't give up, I came up with another idea, why not drive there on our bikes. Doug was interested and I started to gather information on border crossings and currency. Unfortunately my idea was not original, others had tried and had come to grief near Timbuktu; it had made the papers. The people who had never been near anything more dangerous than a pencil sharpener always blow the danger up out of all proportion: Doug was out.

There was a news report about a South African who gathered people together in Algeria and took them through central Africa in convoy. Very voortrekker; I showed the report to Doug but he wouldn't change his mind, he had accepted an offer for his bike and paid for his passage. Eventually he met a Birmingham girl out there and they married; as far as I know he's still there. I am sure we could have done it my way. I had already seen deserts in North Africa but his background was different to mine. We threw a party to see him off and he did me one last favour, he introduced me to a girl he had just met, her name was Jessica Forester.

Chapter 20

Jess

Doug had met this girl at a dance and given her a lift home on his motorbike. He could give me no more information other than that she had just packed in her boy friend, so I didn't know what to expect. We went to the pictures and then it was home to meet her parents. That first meeting with her family was tense; she was their only child and their pride and joy. Her father missed the call up for the war because of his reserved occupation in a factory and in addition, he had worked seven nights a week at a public house from the beginning of the war. For his dedication he had been promised a pub of his own, so he was judging me from the lofty position of a prospective innkeeper; was I good enough for his daughter?

The previous boy friend had been a Communist and had impressed the old man with intellectual, theoretical, left wing, clap trap. In any other circumstances, I would have run for my bike but I really liked this girl, so I persevered. Jess was a short hand typist with a grammar school education and she made it quite clear from the outset that she wasn't going to take any rubbish from me,
"Come up with something sensible and we'll talk about it," was her only concession.
She played the piano and liked classical music, I was crazy about Italian tenors, so what about a trip to London to see an opera.
"We'll tell your dad it's for educational reasons."
She said that was fine but I could forget that part about sharing the same room.
"But it's cheaper that way," I pleaded.
"I'll pay my own way," she countered.
The romance prospered and four operas later and a trip to the Town Hall to see Bengimino Gigli the world

famous tenor, we were talking about an engagement party.

I had to stop tomcatting about at the factory, the Friday night caper was out and the girls gave me a hard time.
"If you're going to bring in an outsider you'll spoil everything."
Jess had the answer, "Leave me or leave the factory."
Now that Doug had gone things were not the same, so leaving was not a problem. Jess worked for the chief buyer at the Hercules Cycle Company and she told me there were two vacancies for toolmakers at the factory. We wouldn't be together, she was in head office several miles away but I went and got the job anyway. The other vacancy was filled by an ex RAF Officer. We became life long friends and he became my tool room foreman when I had my own factory years later.

The Hercules Cycle Company had a bad reputation before the war because they were renowned for sacking dozens of people for no reason. However it had been taken over by a large conglomerate and now it was a first class outfit. They had an excellent welfare service and barbers and dentists were in the works; there were no excuses for having time off. If you were sick, the Welfare Officer visited you at home. That fell foul of the left wing unions who said that they were only spying on us to make sure we were really ill. These lefties made me sick, I was a card carrying young conservative at the time and heckling left wing politicians was par for the course.

I took Jess to some of our party meetings and to some other political rivals, I liked to show off arguing with the speakers but Jess was not impressed,
"I want entertaining not educating."
Bearing in mind what happened to her commie boy-friend, I eased off the political stuff but I must have beaten the commie because when she retired she

became the Conservative chairman of the Parish Council. We perfected our dancing technique in spite of my awkward left foot and often led the floor when the band stuck up.

There was a more serious side which we had to face up to; Jess put it plainly, "Where are we going to live?" I didn't know but I was certain where we were not going to live. Jess told her parents but they couldn't understand. There were two spare bedrooms on offer but I was so adamant that they never mentioned it again. I let Jess have her own way on lots of things but in this matter there was no compromise. Leave home or leave me, touché. We had several false tries on rented property and I turned my attention to emigration again.

The Australia £10 passage was getting a lot of stick in the press, people were returning with horror stories. This didn't put me off, I thought they were losers anyway and I made serious enquiries at Australia House in the town centre. The interview went very well; toolmakers were very much in demand. I had a bit of trouble because I had no papers to prove my ability but letters from firms I worked for would suffice. I enquired about short hand typists and they were even more sort after than toolmakers. Jess was very pleased when I told her. She had plenty of paper proving what she could do. I was having no trouble convincing her that this was the right thing for both of us. It was now a simple case of tying the wedding date to a sailing date. Then came a piece of news that I still bear a grudge about to this day.

"Mom's going to give us the deposit on a house." Jess stopped me dead with those words. I knew that emigration was a secondary consideration to finding somewhere to live but I was now sold on the idea, I also knew that I was being bought.
"Thirty pieces of silver," I said.

"What's the matter with you, aren't you pleased?"

The answer to that was both yes and no and with hindsight it should have been no. It is impossible to explain the difficulties of trying to build a nest when we are the only species on earth that make a problem out of it. In today's terms, I was being offered £30,000 towards the cost of a house. Of course I gave in and have regretted it ever since. Wherever you live you are the same person and I had a few ideas about what to do in Australia. Solar Panels were one scheme. I tried it and I had one operating on my roof ten years before any were available commercially. It failed in the UK to make any money but in Australia it was a runaway success. Who knows what sort of factory I would have finished up with if I had ignored my prospective mother-in-law's offer? Now however, the die was cast and I didn't want to spoil it for Jess. I had done my seven years in the University of Life and I was ready to get married and raise two point four children.

Even with money you are still not free of the men in suits. I fancied a big old house with a cellar and garage; the building societies didn't agree. It must be built after 1930 with no cellar or attic. We finished up with a semi-detached in a row of look-a-likes. With our combined salaries, we could have afforded a much bigger loan but the Society wouldn't budge; they would only take account of my basic wage. It was for my own protection they said. In that, they were right because in later years they broke their own rules and as a result a lot of young people are in financial trouble because of it.

What this proved to me was that there are only three kinds of money:
- got no money
- comfortable money
- up yours money!

Unless you were in the latter bracket, you had to tow the line. This doesn't mean you couldn't be happy; no one could have been more excited than we were. We fixed our wedding date and I moved into the house immediately, with a firm promise to Jess that I wouldn't sleep in the bed until we were married: as an ex army man I couldn't make a problem out of sleeping on the floor. We were married in a High Church by a vicar called Canon Power, a very apt name for a man who joined two people together in such a powerful relationship.

Promotional picture following a major deal with the Nigerian Government.

Seven years later, we sold the house at a profit so that I could start my own business with a part time colleague called Ken, who was a musician. Linking our names together to into Kenton Tools, we formed an engineering firm that eventually became successful, but it was hard at first. Sitting around a coke stove eating beans from a tin can and wondering if any cheques had cleared so that I could have some wages. Ken would turn up at midnight, straight from the dance hall and still in evening dress, to work on the lathe until morning. This perseverance paid off and eventually we exported machine tools all over the world.

Russians at Downing Street. A Russian trade delegation, including the compulsory KGB man visited our works in Downing Street, Smethwick when we signed a £100,000 deal with them in the 1970s

In 1983, we even won the Queen's Award for export. It was cancelled at the last minute because of an error on an invoice. My wife was very upset because she had already kitted up for her visit to Buckingham Palace.

Thirteen years later though we did go to the Palace. I was invited to the Palace Garden Party in 1996 because of my affiliation with the 'Not Forgotten' Club, which is part of the War Pensions Agency. Jess was so excited about being able to dress up but the 1983 costume was no good, she insisted that it was out of date. It was back to Haute Couture all over again as we trawled the fashion shops. On the day, she finished up wearing a costume similar to Princess Margaret and that 'made it all worth the effort': Jess' words, not mine.

Jess and I at Buckingham Palace Garden Party in 1996

Jess and I had a wonderful and happy retirement; we had been together for fifty two years when she died on Good Friday 2001. I only wish she could be here now to read this story about the D-Day Dodger she married.

Mr Albert Darlington, managing director of Kenton Tools (Birmingham Ltd), whose company is in the finals of the business awards competition.

£10,000 fillip for winning company

West Midland firms, whose products range from tools and machinery to furnaces, food, souvenirs and printing, are in the running for a £10,000 business boost.

They are the top contenders for the Small Business Award and could win £5,000 in cash and a rent-free factory in Wolverhampton for a year.

The award, jointly sponsored by the National Girobank and Wolverhampton Enterprise Ltd in association with the Express and Star, is aimed at manufacturing firms employing less than 25 people, but with growth potential.

Wolverhampton accountants Binder Hamlyn have also offered £1,000 worth of free professional services to the winning firm — provided it has no financial advisers already.

Entries for the contest have come from all parts of the West Midlands and six finalists have been selected to face the judging panel.

From Brierley Hill comes Ercal Printing Services, a printing firms set up by partners Jack Brown, David Crook and Ken Bullock six years ago.

Since then, jobs have been found for two machine managers and four youngsters to learn the trade.

Mr Brown said the lease on the premises in North Street expires in March and the chance of a free factory in Wolverhampton, plus £5,000 in cash, would be a "godsend."

Another contender, Kenton Tools of Smethwick also faces the problem of the lease expiring on its Downing Street premises next September.

The company says key personnel would not mind moving to Wolverhampton and the £5,000 would enable two more fitters to be recruited.

Kenton, formed in 1956, employs ten people making special purpose machinery and polishing jigs for everything from artificial hip joints to golf clubs.

It has also opened up export markets in Russia, Nigeria, Egypt and Cyprus.

Fule Conservation Services

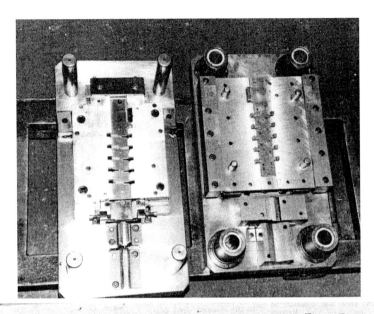

'Downing Street' lands big Russian order

RUSSIANS who dropped in on the "other Downing Street" have signed up a £100,000 job boosting contract with a Smethwick firm.

For the red-carpet visit was to Downing Street . . Smethwick.

The order has resulted in Kenton Tools taking on more staff.

A delegation of Russians, the "managing director" of the company, and two State officials visitied the firm for talks.

Afterwards, Kenton Tools managing director, Mr. Albert Darlington, said the prospects of more business looked good.

It is the second contract with the Russians

that Kentons have won. Five years' ago they supplied machinery worth £70,000 to a Russian motor complex.

Kentons will this time supply know-how and machinery to a State-owned knife and fork-making company. Written instructions alone took up two cwt of paper which had to shipped overseas.

Kentons, which employs 26 people, took on five extra staff at Christmas to cope with the order. It is equivalent

to a year's work for the company.

Mr. Darlington said: "If we secure a third phase of the contract to install machinery and train people how to use it we may be able to take on more staff."

He said the business would be worth a further £150,000.

The sales director, Mr. Ray Jeeves, was today having more talks with the Russians, who are visiting a company in South Wales, to try to swing the deal.

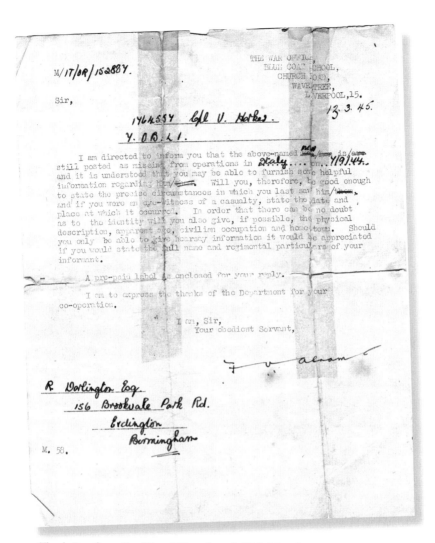

M/17/OR/152884.

THE WAR OFFICE,
BLUE COAT SCHOOL,
CHURCH ROAD,
WAVERTREE,
LIVERPOOL,15.

13. 3. 45.

Sir,

1464554 Cpl V. Harker.
Y.O.B.21.

I am directed to inform you that the above-named man/~~~~ is/~~~~
still posted as missing from operations in Italy.... on..7/9/44.
and it is understood that you may be able to furnish some helpful
information regarding him/~~~~. Will you, therefore, be good enough
to state the precise circumstances in which you last saw him/~~~~,
and if you were an eye-witness of a casualty, state the date and
place at which it occurred. In order that there can be no doubt
as to the identity will you also give, if possible, the physical
description, apparent age, civilian occupation and home town. Should
you only be able to give hearsay information it would be appreciated
if you would state the full name and regimental particulars of your
informant.

A pre-paid label is enclosed for your reply.

I am to express the thanks of the Department for your
co-operation.

I am, Sir,
Your obedient Servant,

R. Darlington Esq
156 Brookvale Park Rd.
Erdington
Birmingham

M. 58.

*The letter from the War Office dated 13th March 1945 asking me if
I knew what had happened to Corporal V Harker. Gordon was blown
up by a grenade right in front of me.*

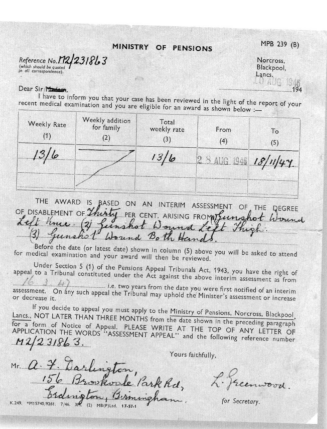

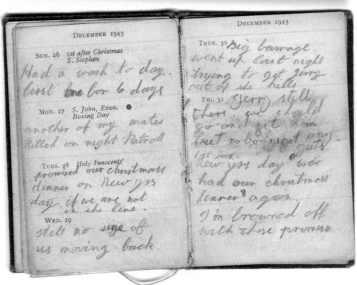

Top: My letter from the Ministry of Pensions reducing my entitlement to 30%. Bottom: Some of my thoughts at the end of 1943.

Acknowledgements

My sincere and many thanks to all the people who have helped to bring this book to life. It has been forty years in the planning, but at last, I have the opportunity to share the experiences of my early life with other people, some of whom went through the same austere years. There will be others though who read this book, for whom the war was no more than a series of gung ho films, a history lesson or the memories of their own relatives. I hope that by reading this story, some of them at least will reflect upon the hardship, the sadness, and the companionship of another generation which won for them the freedoms which they enjoy today.

I would like to thank my daughter Barbara who helped me to put the text onto paper - and into my computer. All the authors whose books and work I have had access to, so that I might clarify my own memories and put them into some context and chronology; the Express & Star, Birmingham Post and Birmingham Mail newspapers for their consent to reproduce various photographs and articles. I am also indebted to the Regimental Archivists of the Oxford and Buckingham Light Infantry at Slade Park for their help, and in particular to Lieutenant Colonel David Stanley, OBE, RD, Lieutenant Colonel Dowden, JP, DL, KCSG and Major PR Hayter, MBE, MC. My thanks also go to Mr KJS Ballantyne, LL.B (Hons), Solicitor, of Laundry Cottage Books for agreeing to publish The D-Day Dodger and for his help and advice along the way. Finally may I thank you, the reader, for buying my book and for giving me the opportunity to donate to the Severn Hospice.

Albert F Darlington

Albert Darlington, by dint of a quick wit, a measure of luck, and the skill of the best of light Infantrymen lived to write this story sixty years or more after the events portrayed took place. Light Infantrymen were taught to think for themselves and use their initiative, which Albert always did, sometimes to the extent that it got him into trouble as well as out of it.

By this mix of skill and luck Albert managed to survive all the actions fought by the 7th Battalion, The Oxfordshire and Buckinghamshire Light Infantry, in the Italian Campaign. To do so was no mean feat since the 7th Battalion won more Battle Honours and suffered more casualties than any other Battalion of the Regiment in the war. Fighting through very difficult and rugged terrain, in frequent close contact with highly trained and professional German soldiers, Italy was certainly not what Churchill had described as 'the soft underbelly of Europe'. It is hardly surprising that Albert's experiences took their toll upon him and that he was twice seriously wounded; what is surprising is that he survived at all.

Albert paints a vivid, unique and at times harrowing picture of war as seen through the eyes of a private soldier. Had he been prepared to accept promotion, I have no doubt that he would have risen through the ranks. His description of the early days of the War as a sixteen year old from a hard family background, and of post war privations provide a fascinating insight into a Britain which has gone forever.

My generation, which followed behind in the fifties, will always be eternally grateful for what he and his like sacrificed for us.

David Stanley, Lt Colonel (Ret'd), OBE, RD
Oxfordshire and Buckinghamshire
Light Infantry Museum

Bibliography

Once There Was a War
John Steinbeck
William Heinemann 1959

World Almanac of World War 2
edited by Peter Young
Bison Books Ltd 1981

Rome '44
Raleigh Trevelyan
Martin Secker & Warburg 1981

Cassino, The Hollow Victory
John Ellis
London Sphere 1985

Mutiny at Salerno
Saul David
Brassey's, London 1995

Monte Cassino
Matthew Parker
Headline Book Publishing 2003

Three Counties Asylum
Judith Pettigrew,
Rory W Reynolds
and Sandra Rouse 1998

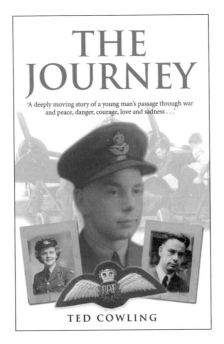

THE JOURNEY

'A deeply moving story of a young man's passage through war and peace, danger, courage, love and sadness . . .'

TED COWLING

IN this true, fascinating and very moving story, Ted Cowling takes the reader through his childhood to his enlistment into the RAF on 4th September 1939. He describes his brushes with death in the skies over occupied Europe and his part in a top secret and highly dangerous mission to Russia in 1941, upon which the course of the Second World War turned.

In 1944 he saved the lives of his crew and was awarded the Distinguished Flying Cross "For courage and devotion to duty on active service whilst flying against the enemy". He became a 'Top Gun' instructor and married the beautiful young WAAF who one night saved his life. After the RAF he entered the world of the entrepreneur. Success followed but with it desperate tragedy and sadness.